Run Toward the Roar

*Transform Crisis and Change into the
Opportunity to Thrive*

John R. Robertson

Published by Prominence Publishing, www.prominencepublishing.com

Edited By: Barb Kelly, Subject Matters Canada.

The author can be reached as follows: info@fortlog.co

Run Toward the Roar/John R. -- 1st ed.

ISBN: 978-1-988925-89-9

Dedication

To Carolyn, our three children – William, Chris, and Amanda – and our son-in-law Matt, who have taught me so much through their questioning, and provided support and inspiration by modelling what it means to thrive despite the challenges life has thrown them.

And, to Elaine, gone from sight but not from my heart, who saw this content in a book before I even believed in it.

Acknowledgements

I want to express my deep gratitude to Carolyn and our four children, who believed in me when I stopped believing in myself or this book. They challenged and encouraged me and told others what I was working on, even though I would have preferred no one else knew. It is their support that allowed me to be resilient in this effort even when, so many times, I wanted to just quit and walk away.

I need to acknowledge Barb, my editor, who has become a friend, for the lion's share (pun intended) of work and perseverance to bring this to fruition. The work that she did to enable the content to have some sensibleness, even when I did not like what she recommended, clarified what I wanted to say. I have learned so often that the things needed most may not be what we always want to hear. Thank you, Barb.

I am so grateful for those who allowed me to work this ethos with them and so many others who support the work I do. I cannot begin to name you all. I will let you know personally when we speak as I am truly blessed for your backing, reassurance, and the times when I have been told to *suck it up and just start rowing!*

I also want to thank my niece and her family, who have shown what resilience and thriving mean throughout her cancer journey. I have seen, and learned from watching, what happens when values are clear and lived when the right supports are in place. Their Run Toward the Roar mindset has continued when sometimes it must have felt like it would be easier to give up instead of pressing on.

Table of Contents

Foreword

I never knew much about crisis management.

As a business owner I would simply fix problems as they arose, until I found out the hard way that just because a problem is fixable, doesn't mean the crisis is over. In many cases, fixing the "problem" has little to do with resolving the crisis.

I never knew much about values either.

I always just operated my business according to what I felt was right at the time. But I found that I often struggled to make decisions in the moment based on what I felt was right. And sometimes I made decisions that caused negative repercussions.

I never understood the difference between an event and a crisis, nor did I understand the importance of values...until I met John.

In these pages is wisdom that could literally save your business millions of dollars, or maybe even save your business...period!

John's extensive experience and profound wisdom regarding crisis management will teach you how to tell the difference between the event and the crisis, how to respond to both and how to avoid both.

This book will remind you of some common sense that you may be taking for granted. More importantly, it will reveal what I call "uncommon sense"; ideas, principles, strategies, and techniques you have never considered before which will not only prepare you with the tools you need to respond to crises, but the wisdom you need to avert them altogether.

I challenge you, dear reader, to not only read these pages, but explore them with an open mind. Set aside that which you think you already know and clear the way for new knowledge because within these pages is valuable foresight.

Steve Lowell, CSP

President, Global Speakers Federation
Award-Winning International Speaker
2x #1 International Best-Selling Author
Co-Founder of "Deep Thought Strategy" and "The Perfect Sales System"

Preface

Do you get tired of hearing or seeing normal people with normal reactions being treated as abnormal?

I know I do. After a bus crash, a tornado, or a shooting, after a significant event, when people show that they are nervous, in fear, or in tears – why is that a problem?

Often people displaying a normal reaction to an unexpected event end up apologizing for their reaction. Why are they apologizing? For being human? It's no wonder mental health concerns are on the rise!

People keep asking me where it is written that they maintain a level-headed, rational state during a crisis rather than being human.

This book is my way of reframing things. What would happen if we defined a positive, a new norm? What would happen if we each defined an individual destiny toward which we each became faithful and grew?

People face crises. What if we learned how to thrive through disasters? What if – instead of reacting or suppressing what's inside – we took advantage of our human abilities and learned to respond?

I went to university to be a doctor (I did not make it very far), so I am not criticizing our medical model of health, but sometimes I wonder if our definitions of health, thriving, resilience, and well-being are more often *not sick* rather than a positive, realistic mindset of *being healthy*? Sometimes it seems we are human *doings* rather than human *beings*.

Have you ever struggled with what you know you should do versus what you are more comfortable doing? Or, worse, knowing what you should do but not doing it until you are so sick you *must* do it. I sure have.

I have long wondered why so many people talk about resilience, mental health, and other related themes, yet when it comes to implementation, they fail to have long-term success.

Have you ever wanted something so badly that you were willing to do almost anything to achieve it? I smile as I type this because one man I asked answered, "Yes!" and then clarified that he wanted hair, but he was still bald.

So aside from hair, think about wants you valued so much that you worked and persevered, even when it would have been easier to stop or quit.

For these outcomes you valued so deeply, the choice was a long- or short-term ethos – or mindset – and that makes the difference between wanting something and achieving it.

I have spent over 30 years working in transforming crisis – with businesses ranging in size from one employee to several hundred – and two things are constant: 1.) dealing with change and 2.) change can be the crisis for some. In other words, dealing with change. Since the event itself is never the real crisis but one's reaction or response to it, I've learned that people must define a new norm after a crisis to grow forward afterward.

People who have clear values tend to grow through events in more proactive and healthier ways than those who do not, even when it is brutally challenging to do so. Those who live without clear values and, thus, react rather than respond to a crisis, discover, often too late, what their values should have been prior to the crisis happening.

What if we explore thriving as a discussion about faithfulness or loyalty, where one is committed to living their convictions, their values. The US Marines have adopted the motto *Semper Fidelis*, yet the Latin is not theirs alone. These two words translate to mean *always faithful*, or *always loyal*.

What if we took the time to define what we are loyal to, faithful to, to develop a theme of faithfulness to our values? In other words, is it realistic to describe thriving and resilience by being faithful to something regardless of the cost? I believe it is.

I have seen it in injured athletes who return to their sport against all odds. I have worked with non-athletes who get walloped by an event that completely takes them out of their game, yet they find a way to get back into it. And I have worked with people for whom the effort, faithfulness, and discipline needed to get back in the game were more than they were willing to do at the time.

Passio fidelis is a term I've made up using Latin. *Passio* is the root word for passion. This passion means to suffer, endure, undergo, and/or experience. Wouldn't you say that is a valid term for resilience and thriving? The second word, *fidelis* means fidelity, which is the foundation of trust, loyalty, allegiance, devotion, and faithfulness. I think this term encompasses valuable qualities, don't you? As you read this book, remember *passio fidelis*.

The tough work ahead of us is to define and refine our values. No one else can do this work for us and we can't just hope-wish-pray-dream and have values.

Values that are anchored around convictions are ones about which we are so thoroughly convinced something is absolutely true that we'll take a stand for it regardless of the consequences. A key theme that we'll delve into in this work – standing *for* something – is not about reacting or being *against* something but being motivated by whom or what we are *for*.

I believe people are naturally resilient, so why not strengthen what is natural and consider it more thoroughly? People say that a crisis can be an opportunity, but this is not a given. Crisis can be a chance to do new things or do old things in a new way.

Imagine living a focussed, passionate commitment toward your deepest values, regardless of the roars along the way. What would happen if you determined some things that you could be passionate about and faithful to that required a sense of unwavering commitment?

Thrive in the way that matters to you!

Some of the greatest people in your life may not have been world icons; I know this is true in my life. Consider reframing success into a *passio fidelis* that matters and lasts. And I want the people around me to feel better for it – what about you?

Introduction

This book presents a values-anchored ethos – based in one's passion and loyalty – that ensures one thrives through crises and changes. Too many of us react to life stressors by succumbing, fighting, avoiding, or hiding, which leads to a life that is controlled solely by stressors and is no fun at all. If you believe we are on this earth to lead mundane, even miserable, lives, stop reading now, because this book is not for you. If, however, you believe we can live rewarding, fulfilling lives – even with stressors as constant challenges – then read on, my friend, read on.

This approach involves understanding that our responses to fear are learned behaviors, which can be changed, rather than automatic reactions that must always remain the same.

It will take some work to alter our reaction and response to crisis and change – nothing of great value in this life comes easily -- but once you define a mindset you are committed to, dealing with crises and changes will become second nature and thriving will be the result. The work will come in the form of exercises and writings in the accompanying Run Toward The Roar Discovery Guide (available at www. runtowardtheroar.online/discoveryguide) in which you will examine your past and present behaviors, beliefs, and values to determine if they are helpful or harmful when dealing with stressors and writings in which you re-define, refine, and clarify what you are committed to as you grow forward.

You will see in this book two metaphors that represent stressors or crises in our lives – the roar of a lion and the roar of hazards like white-water rapids in a river on which we are travelling – although one is concise and one is ongoing, both are dangerous and instill fear in our souls. Both can be dealt with successfully by running toward them rather than following any of our natural reactions or responses to threats.

What represents a roar in one person's life may be different than what represents a roar in another's; however, we all face roars, whether due to environmental causes (hurricanes, earthquakes, landslides, tidal waves, etc.) or human causes (accidents, sewer back-ups, a lack of leadership, toxic workplaces, unemployment, family issues, etc.).

It is important to learn how to deal with roars in a thoughtful, unwavering way – either before or after the initial roar. Doing so is the only way to thrive, or live with passion, rather than enduring, resisting, or succumbing to the roar.

Use this book – read and re-read sections as you need – write in the margins and blank areas, fold the Run Toward the Roar Discovery Guide and a journal or notebook inside the cover and carry them together. Re-answer and re-write questions for different, difficult situations you are facing. In time, your new ethos (convictions) and responses will become entrenched in who you are and how you live so that you can thrive rather than merely survive.

PART I

The Roar

Having worked in crisis intervention and mental health for over 30 years, there is a consistent theme that troubles me: Why do so many of us keep reacting and repeatedly doing the same things? Why do we spend time and money on things that we think will improve our lives, but which still leave us feeling like something is missing? Despite everything we do, we are not fulfilled and are not living a rewarding life. We are not thriving.

Thriving is more than just being the one with the most toys, the most money, the most accomplishments, the most friends, the most fans, or the most power. Since we are not taking it with us, how does accumulating things and influence have any final satisfaction to it?

I have yet to meet a person who does not want to thrive; to have made a difference that no one else – let me repeat, *no one else* – could ever make and money could never buy... to live in such a way that life's hazards and hurdles do not stop us even though they might slow us down or cause a detour. It is not money, things, or influence that help us thrive; it is our passion and loyalty for the relationship with ourself, our values, our commitments, our integrity, our desires, and our relationships that help us thrive.

Roars are crises, fears, unpleasant events, obstacles, and storms that occur in our life. These events are powerful enough to generate the normal reactions of fight, flight, appease, or freeze. But those reactions – while allowing us to survive – often don't involve positive thinking (they are based in fear), let alone positive results (we survive, yes, but do we thrive?).

What would happen if, instead of instinctually reacting to roars, we chose our responses to roars? What if we prepared ourselves so that instead of reacting to the roars, we were able to choose our response based on something other than fear and do something different. What if our response was based on our understanding of ourself, our values, our goals, and our practices, so we moved toward the roar, addressed it, and thrived as a result?

Isn't it ironic that the US Marines, and so many others, speak about faithfulness and loyalty, yet mental health professionals regularly don't? I am not talking about imposing one's faith or loyalties onto another (that's immoral), but those working in mental health professions need to discuss and bring the discussion of faithfulness to one's values into the conscious field of operation.

After searching through numerous sources over the years, I cannot find any definition of faith that includes religion. Yes, there are many meanings discussing faith and belief, but I have never found faith defined as religion.

A person can follow all the rules and practices and be very religious and still not have faith; and a person can have faith and not practice religious rituals or customs at all. When using the term faith while reading this book, doing the work, and practising running toward the roar, it does not necessarily mean religion. In the book Honor Bound, Stuart Rochester and Frederick Kiley state, "There is virtually no personal account in the Vietnam Prisoner of War (POW) literature that does not contain some reference to a transforming spiritual episode."[1] This is the outcome of faith – a spiritual transformation – not a religious one.

This book is *not* the story of a super, world-renowned person named John Robertson who has overcome some significant crises. However, I can tell you I have had my share of roars, storms, and crises, of issues and hurdles to overcome, and this much is true: I am thriving, I am in the game, and I am finishing well because I have chosen to Run Toward the Roar (RTTR).

Over the decades of this work, I have served a variety of people, but I love the personalized results. One nurse I was working with was burning out in her workplace, getting overlooked for any promotions, and yet being given more and more responsibilities. If she looked at leaving her job, it would cost her her pension, seniority, and many other things. Her passion and values were all around being a nurse though. We walked through RTTR and, as a result, she is now working in a senior's residence, including palliative care support. I received a message from her saying she loves what she is doing. The people are allowing her to lead and use her strengths. The only regret she has is that she should have done it years ago.

In these early chapters of the book, I'm inviting you to examine your own thinking. To define or refine some core abstract terms that can be ambiguous, and to define your destiny so you navigate toward it, despite the storms that may cross your path. I am also challenging you to look at relationships with yourself and others to determine who will support you and who you will support and serve to assist with their storms to build your thriving community.

Thriving must be rooted in your definition of success and anchored in your community in which the members breathe life into one another. It is a values-anchored approach where your course is set by your values, passions, courage, ethos, and -- yup – that four-letter word – discipline.

CHAPTER ONE

Reaction Versus Response

We all know the lion is the King of the jungle. He is feared by all animals, including humans, and when he roars, all react in one of four ways: challenging the lion, running away from him, staying motionless and hoping the lion will not notice them, or doing what the lion wants -- usually while cowering, cringing, or sulking.

Through all reactions, the lion continues his reign of the jungle. How? He continues to roar, creating crises for all those on the receiving end of his threat. He instinctually knows that his roars cause reactions and responses that rarely alter and are one of four – fight, flight, freeze, or appease.

Reactions To Fear

Faced with a roar, all animals – including humans – experience fear immediately and first. It is woven into our DNA and spurs us on to survive threats to our safety, well-being, and life. Also woven into our DNA are four responses to fear and, within milliseconds of experiencing a threat, animals feel fear and select and initiate their response.

Fight

Those that feel they can challenge the lion will respond by fighting him. Understandably, few choose this option unless all other options are unavailable (for example, if the lion is so close that flight, freezing, or appeasing are not options). A hunter with a rifle may choose to try to shoot the lion; this is a form of fighting. Other animals, a tiger, or a pack of hyenas, may try to fight and distract the lion to try and steal a small portion of a kill, but this is not always successful.

Flight

Those who are far enough away or fast enough may choose to run away from the lion until they are safe. Flight can also be a response that occurs after an animal tries fighting a lion (if they survive). It is the most common reaction in the animal world. Fleeing is often the most life-preserving response to a threat.

Freeze

Freezing is often the choice of an animal that is not very fast, is too close to the lion to run, or has not yet fully comprehended the threat. You've heard the expression, "A deer in headlights." This is a reference to the propensity of deer to freeze in the middle of the road when a car's headlights suddenly shines toward them at night. Small animals, not easily noticed, often have this response as well. They freeze and stay very still until the threat has passed, hoping the predator will not see them or will see another animal that is a more interesting meal.

Appease

This is often the choice of members of the lion's pride. They tend to do what the lion wants them to do when he roars at them. They may be cowering, resentful, frustrated, sulking, or cringing as they do it, but they do it, nevertheless. Cubs trying to play with the lion often respond this way when the lion roars to send them away. Young lions and lionesses in the pride may also behave this way when the alpha lion claims their share of a kill as his own.

Through all challenges, the lion continues his reign of the jungle by continuing to roar and create crises for all those around him.

React Versus Respond

The difference between an animal's reaction to a lion's roar and a human's response to a crisis is that animals can only react in one of four ways – fight, flight, freeze, or appease – while humans, although initially reacting in one of those ways, have the reasoning mind (the frontal cortex) that can assess the roar as only that: a roar. Not a crisis. Rather than the instantaneous reactions of the jungle animals, we can choose to *respond* in any way, and we can choose to survive, to persist, or to thrive.

Tragically, when it comes to crises (changes, trials, struggles, or other stresses) all that most of us hear is the roar. People start everything – including each day – with great hopes, but when they hit a hurdle and stumble or begin to get stressed or meet something unexpected, they become fearful because the roar of the challenge frightens them and they react instinctually (fight, flight, freeze, or appease).

The world has always roared, but the roars are more numerous and more frequent today – particularly with advancements in technology and communications – so the roars are non-stop and primal reactions are more common amongst people of all ages because fears are rising throughout humanity. For example, the elderly fear that they will lose their good health or retirement income; those in their prime income-making years fear job loss or that they will never earn enough money to retire; younger generations worry they will never own a home or have a family, while others fear the environment will kill them before they should die, and many fear their partner will become dissatisfied or distracted and leave. In all age demographics, the Fear of Missing Out (FOMO) exists.

Rather than sharing an example from personal experience, I need to share the impact that the power of FOMO is having on the wellbeing and resilience of young people. The Royal Society for Public Health (RSPH)[2] released a study on social media and young people's mental health and wellbeing.[3]

They surveyed people between the ages of 14-24. Their findings offered a clear picture of how different social media platforms impact mental health issues, including anxiety, depression, sleep deprivation, and body-image. While there were some positive effects, a summary of the study states:

> *Instagram was found to have the most negative overall effect on young people's mental health. The popular photo sharing app negatively impacts body image and sleep, increases bullying and "FOMO" (fear of missing out), and leads to greater feelings of anxiety, depression, and loneliness.*
>
> **Facebook** *was found to have similar negative effects to Instagram in the categories of bullying, FOMO, body image, anxiety, depression, and loneliness. Facebook also has a particularly negative impact on sleep.*

Our primal reactions to fear – fight, flight, freeze, or appease – are automatic reflexes, so all living things initially react in one of these ways -- there is no thinking involved – the reactions have been hardwired into us since our primitive beginnings. But humans are uniquely able to override these impulses using memories of past experiences, rational thought, training, and practice.

I'm not suggesting we pretend there is nothing to fear or that we think only positive thoughts. I am not saying all we need to do is show no fear. That would be foolish and deny human nature. It is the moment between perception and reaction, between reaction and action, that we can separate ourselves from the other species. We can train ourselves to ignore our initial reaction to fight, flee, freeze, or appease and, instead, respond by running *toward* the roars.

Look at it another way: Don't we have enough to fear in this world? In our rapidly changing world, there are so many things that are no longer certain: jobs, retirement, relationships, health, the definition of families, all are changing rapidly. We can't survive, let alone enjoy life, if we are constantly reacting to these challenges by fighting, fleeing, freezing, or appeasing. Not just because our life will be unhappy but also because people will take advantage of us.

Some leverage our fears to their advantage. This is what happens during a hot sellers' market in real estate. The fear of missing out on a home impels a buyer to bid higher than one would normally offer. This, in turn, can start a bidding war. Some realtors play on this FOMO. The seller and her/his realtor list the property for less than its actual market value. They then set a date by which interested buyers must submit an offer. The seller can then choose from the blind offers the buyers have submitted and – of course – choose the highest bid that comes in, which is usually well over the property's market value. The bidders' FOMO drives their bid decisions rather than rational thought.

Many had the same feeling about toilet paper at the start of the COVID-19 pandemic. Many saw others buying loads of it and began to feel an irrational FOMO that they were missing something and, thus, bought loads, as well.

My family regularly pokes fun at me because I always have extra toilet paper on hand, but even I was wondering if I should buy more at the beginning of the pandemic. So, if I – the well-stocked toilet paper guy – am feeling FOMO, imagine the impact on someone with FOMO who doesn't stock up ahead of needing it.

The point is, I didn't fall into the primal reflex to buy more toilet paper when I felt the impulse to do so. I used my rational mind to think about the situation and reasoned that even if there was a shortage of toilet paper, I had more than enough paper on hand to deal with it.

The Myopic Life

Sadly, when it comes to crises, changes, trials, struggles, or other stresses, all that most of us hear is the roar. People start everything – including each day – with great hopes, but when they hit a hurdle and stumble or begin to get stressed or meet something unexpected, they become fearful because the roar of the challenge frightens them and they react instinctually (fight, flight, freeze, or appease) and react with nearsightedness! It is impossible to thrive while only seeing and doing something about the issues directly in front of us at the expense of bigger, longer-term issues and goals.

There is a human eye condition called myopia; it is also known as nearsightedness. I know about it because I have it. People with myopia are unable to focus on distant objects. The cure is relatively simple: corrective lenses. However, as a person who despises wearing glasses, I find this a dilemma. I could go through life never clearly seeing anything other than a few feet in front of me or I can be an adult, do the right thing, and wear the lenses needed to see!

There are those – even with 20/20 vision – who live a myopic life. They believe that urgent issues are important issues. Urgent issues are those that need immediate attention and action while important issues are those of great significance or value. Some people have trouble making the distinction between urgent and important issues and focus only on the urgent ones. In this myopic state, they are so busy dealing with what's right in front of them each day that they fail to see anything in the distance and fail to identify the values and goals most important to them. These people see urgent things as roars and have trouble getting past daily chores and events because they are consumed with daily roars.

We all know people who live myopically. We listen to them talk about their busy-ness. Everything is urgent. Most things are crises, as one roar builds upon the last for them. For example, one morning they can't find their keys, which immediately puts them into a tailspin as they frantically look for the missing keys and -- without a conscious thought -- they are in the myopic mindset. Rather than using the spare set of keys in the kitchen drawer, they are intent on finding the missing keys. This event causes them to completely forget to take a meat out of the freezer for supper (a roar they will hear later in the day when they realize their error). They eventually leave for work late, without their lunch (another future roar). They arrive at work in a tense state only to discover that they are without all the information they worked on the entire previous evening. And so on ... each day of their life seems to go this way.

This myopia may lead them to be curt with others and they may say hurtful things. They neither realize their words are hurtful nor do they remember what they said a day or two later. Indeed, people operating at this level of stress may not realize what they have said or done even immediately after they say or do it.

The result of ongoing, myopic thinking is that the person becomes more controlling and tries to manage every detail of their life because everything is a crisis for them. They are so intense that others don't want to be around them because the myopic can't relax!

Instead of asking, "What's the worst that could happen?" when a roar occurs, these folks immediately focus on *only* the worst that could happen and believe it is inevitably going to occur. They stay near-sighted. This thinking becomes a habit and gets worse as they bounce from one issue to the next until the worst does happen, and they can't bear the stress of it.

Their motion is more side to side as they bounce from fear to fear rather than moving forward with any direction, purpose, or passion toward any goals.

Not only individuals but communities, and organizations, too, can suffer from myopic thinking. One tragedy that I have experienced several times occurs where our work is being done. Working with a company, group or individual, we have started to define their new norm and what healthy will mean for them. Then a crisis happens, even the Covid pandemic, and creates a tyranny of the urgent mindset. People are going in all directions, super busy, but not going anywhere on purpose. The result is that key leadership are now so focussed on reacting to crises, issues, and problems that all forward momentum has stopped. Personnel (and personal) conflicts, power struggles, high turnover, numerous stress leaves, and poor staff morale are all symptoms that prevail when leadership is busy putting out little fires all day, every day, rather than setting goals and measuring the group's progress toward those goals. And, eventually, there will be a big crisis that will knock the organization off its feet.

At an individual level, dealing with the urgent at the cost of the important can be more concerning because the impact ripples into so many other areas of the myopic life, including healthy relationships, work performance, social interactions, and self-care, to name a few.

Many may think it is normal and a good way to look at life, myopically focusing on the immediate issues at hand without looking out into the world or at a neighbor's life to see what they are dealing with. The problem arises when a crisis over which people have no control hits – like the COVID-19 pandemic, for example. Then a huge ROAR is felt: That significant, defining moment when up becomes down and down becomes up, and everything that you were focussed on just evaporates right before your myopic eyes.

Don't get me wrong, this myopic approach is useful – even critical – when a roar first sounds. The myopic response is common when people are initially dealing with a crisis. But there is something very important to remember: The event is never the real crisis. Each person may experience the same event very differently. What one person may find to be a crisis, another may just find to be a bother. It is how you and I react-respond to an event that determines whether short-sighted thinking will consume us. To survive in life-threatening situations, we must focus on the urgent. It is human nature to become nearsighted. In fact, it is based on our biology.

A person in crisis cannot think long-term because our body automatically reacts to the crisis by producing more cortisol (the stress hormone). Increased cortisol suppresses the ability to think long-term and plan. This is why stressed people sometimes say and do things they would normally never do; they are not thinking about the long-term consequences of their actions. It's the body's way of protecting itself. However, this way of dealing with crisis is very physically and psychologically unhealthy in the long run.

When we are in crisis, choosing to respond rather than simply react becomes an exceptionally difficult thing to do. Stress overrides long-range thinking and, as a result, because we are always reacting rather than responding, we get spun in all different directions and end up going nowhere, but we are surviving.

The metaphor I offer for this survival state is the feeling one has when taking amusement rides like the *Teacup*, the *Tilt-a-Whirl*, or the *Scrambler*. These rides involve spinning on at least two axes. One spin comes from the individual seat or car you're in and the other spin comes from the whole ride spinning like a giant turntable. If a car spins a lot, some people in it want off, some get giddy, and some may even get sick (I was the one getting sick). For most people, once the ride ends, leaving can be challenging. One's balance is off, so their walk can look a little like they are drunk. Sometimes, this dizziness feels like it is going to stop us from traveling forward. When life roars and puts us in a spin, it's exiting the spin that sometimes stops us from moving forward.

"Roars come in many forms."

Roars come in many forms – every person has their own unique set of stressors – but the result can be the same sensation, that of spinning around till we are dizzy then struggling to walk forward; having to focus on the few feet in front of us rather than looking further ahead to see the whole fair. But, when we do start to move, the dizziness will fade, and we can focus on what we will do next.

Changing Our Response to The Roar

Humans are the only animals that can use conditioning with reason when we face a frightening roar. Rather than following our primitive instincts to fight, flee, freeze, or appease, we can train ourselves to recognize our fear and respond to a roar differently. We can learn to focus not only on the urgent (survival) but can choose to focus on the important (life), as well. We can choose to run *toward* the roar and not simply survive but *thrive*, instead.

Humans are uniquely built to be able to override our primitive impulses by considering our past experiences and values, training, and practice. For some professionals, this practice is called developing *muscle memory*. Developing muscle memory involves preventing our actions from being determined by our reaction to a crisis; instead, we re-train our mind and body to do something else.

This is what emergency personnel train for. It is why firefighters, police, and ambulance personnel rush <u>towards</u> most places that people are rushing <u>from</u>. They are trained to do that. They are prepared – through regular training sessions, real experiences with fires and emergencies, and their personal values – to run *toward* the crisis and to do everything they can to save others, even at the risk of losing their own lives.

That preparedness is what this book is all about: Re-training the way we respond when facing a roar (crisis) and growing through it. To re-train, we will be guided by our values and our commitment to them will motivate us to define and enact a refined response that will allow us to thrive rather than simply survive.

A Different Approach

A basic requirement for all animals is the need to feel or be safe and secure. It is the most basic need we share. But isn't the reality of safety and security in this world an illusion? Just when we think we have established safety, something always changes or threatens it.

I am proposing that by running toward the roar you find focus and lean forward with conviction and faithfulness. That way, even when life knocks you around, you will fall forward rather than backward or into a heap in the same spot. This is true in any part of life, to live a fulfilling life focussing on goals is more important than the roars – indeed it can overcome them.

To expand this, think of the little things in life that can take you off your game, sometimes without very much effort. Let me illustrate and risk criticism.

My wife and I have three children (she says she has four: three she gave birth to and one she married!). All three are very good athletes and the two boys are now at the age where I can easily lose when we play golf. Since I don't like losing, I have tried to find subtle ways to interrupt their focus – to take them off their game.

You may think this is unfair of me, but I am applying the RTTR principle to my fear of being beaten by my boys (yes, this is a roar for me). The only way I can beat them now is by taking their focus off their goal of winning and get them worried about what might happen (creating a roar for them).

I wish them well, but I also plant doubt in their minds. For example, when they are getting ready to tee off, I say simple things like, "I hope you hit the ball a mile down the fairway and it doesn't just dribble off the tee," or "I hope your ball goes straight as an arrow for you and doesn't hook into the woods," or "I hope your ball doesn't drop into the water on you." And, when they are putting, things like, "I hope you drop the ball right in the hole, not just short of the lip." Of course, they must find this helpful, right? NOT! Quite often the very thing I caution them about actually happens: their ball dribbles off the tee, hooks into the woods, sinks in the pond, or stops just short of the hole. And, they get mad at me, as if it is my fault!

A line from the movie *Seven Days in Utopia* summarizes it perfectly:

> *The toughest issue isn't the golf course or your competitor, it's that casual comment from someone, anyone, about how you should be doing it. If you do not have conviction about what your foundation is, that comment will take you out of your game and erode your confidence.* [4]

The first step in running toward the roar is to define *your values*. It is the faith in, or unwavering commitment to, your values that initiates and strengthens your run forward, toward the roar, rather than fostering the fear that keeps so many stuck in reactions.

Your unwavering commitment – or faithfulness – to your values acts like a harness that you lean into, so you move forward with your load. Those values and your commitment to them are both your motivation for action and your safety mechanism when the road gets rough, just like a harness on a horse ensures the load is moved and stable while moving. Your goals are represented by the open frontier (or destiny) you're striving for, and your values keep you moving in the right direction. At the heart of growing forward and thriving is being able to lean into the harness (your values) to move things toward your open frontier (your destiny), regardless of what anyone else might think.

Another way to look at it is to envision both your faith (unwavering commitment) and your fears (roars) as guideposts along the river of life. Your fears are channel-marking buoys along the shore of the river and mark hazards under the water. They represent the maximum that you can go off-course as you travel along the river, for if you go beyond them or hit the hazard that they mark, you will either run aground or perish. Your unwavering commitment to your values (your faith) determines the route you will follow and acts as a compass used to arrive at your destiny, which is your goal or goals. We must pay attention to three things: buoys (your fears), the compass (your values), and the destiny you're reaching for (your goals) to keep moving forward.

If we focus only on the buoys, we may fall into the myopic life, and bounce back-and-forth across the river between fears (which involves lots of travel but very little forward movement toward our destiny). We may end up paddling on only one side of the boat and we may circle around to move away from our goals rather than toward them. However, we also cannot ignore the buoys. If we do, we are likely to crash into one or more and start taking on water and eventually sink.

> *"And when at some future date the high court of history sits in judgment on each of us ... will be measured by the answers to four questions:*
> *First, were we truly men [women] of courage...*
> *Second, were we truly men [women] of judgment...?*
> *Third, were we truly men [women] of integrity...?*
> *Finally, were we truly men [women] of dedication?"*
> *– John F. Kennedy, 1961*

If we focus only on the compass, we will lose sight of our destiny and buoys. Like focussing too much on the buoys, we may end up treading water, moving backward, crashing and sinking, or sailing toward nothing at all (although it will be with determination).

If we focus only on the destiny, we will be completely unable to deal with the hazards we encounter along the shoreline and beneath the water. We will see our goals, but we will never achieve them because we are ignoring our compass and the river hazards that will set us back or stop us completely.

We must be aware of the buoys (our fears), the compass (our values), and the destiny (our goals) so that we keep moving forward on the river rather than bouncing back and forth, running ashore, going under, or paddling on one side of the boat only and circling in one place.

The first step in RTTR is to identify your values (your compass) for you can't move or change anything without having a compass to determine your path. We'll start with that in the next chapter.

For now, I encourage you to take some time to start identifying your fears and reactions to fears by completing the Chapter One exercises in the RTTR Discovery Guide (www.runtowardtheroar.online/discovery-guide)

CHAPTER TWO

Principles for Progress

Neuroscientists have been using technology to try to measure our *free will* for some time. While opinions about the accuracy of the measurements and the interpretation of the data are wide, there is an interesting theory, developed by Benjamin Libet, that suggests that humans do not have *free will*; we have *free won't*.[5]

In a series of studies over 30 years ago, Libet determined that the urge to act is preceded by electrical activity in the movement area of the brain. He deduced that the brain initiated our actions rather than our free will. This meant, because our brain initiated an action before we chose to act, we could not choose *to* move but could only choose *not to* do something.[6] Of course, this phenomenon occurred in less than half a second, which indicates how complicated studying our *free will* and *free won't* is.

However, when we are looking at our innate reactions and our reasoned responses, it seems that Libet's conclusion applies. For our desire to fight, flee, freeze, or appease is so quick that we can't possibly be choosing our reaction; all we can choose is *not* to follow the urge. It is in the tiniest milliseconds that we must choose not to react but to respond to a roar. Our innate reactions are normal actions taken by a normal person to an abnormal event. So, if our reactions are normal, why should we worry about responding according to our values or our destiny when we are acting on a roar?

Because we can!

We have more cognitive ability than any other animal. Our ability to thrive is far above our primitive reactions. We can store and retrieve memories and use cognitive reasoning to respond in better ways than primitive reactions allow. We were built to do more than just survive or succumb to life. We were built to thrive: To grow, to develop, to flourish, to strengthen, to be healthy, to learn, to live a fulfilling life, whatever our definition of fulfilling may be.

All other species have normal reactions to roars; humans can choose something different than their initial reaction (even when we may not want to).

Think about any movie you have enjoyed versus the ones that fall flat. The movies we enjoy are those in which the characters are challenged by life's adversity. There is a roar where they either fight, flee, freeze (these are usually minor characters or extras who die or are injured or scared away) or appease the villain (these are minor characters who choose to side with the villain to stay alive), or choose to RTTR (the main character always chooses this eventually). Everyone has bad things happen. I am proposing that since everyone has roars in life, it is the response, not the reaction, that matters.

This is thriving: to choose a response different than our innate reaction so we not only bounce back from the roar but grow past our norm to be even better than we were.

I'll be the first to tell you that I was trusting, hoping, wishing, praying for my destiny to happen rather than defining, building, and planning it. To be fair, it is easier to take the path of least resistance. To appease, to take flight, to freeze, or fight things that should not even matter. It's so much easier to blame and play the victim ("...life or other people are to blame for what is happening to me") rather than take responsibility for your life and to RTTR. I know it is sure easier for me to adopt the myopic lifestyle.

I love what Donald Miller of StoryBrand says about this:

> *"I have learned that fate is a terrible writer, if you are trusting your life to fate it is probably not going to go well. Fate is what people call it when they don't want to be responsible for their own journey."*[7]

So, what is a RTTR mindset? It involves using your values to define your destiny, so you thrive rather than just live from one reaction to the next and hope your life ends up where you want.

There is another theory that ties into Libet's idea that we have free won't and our choice to respond rather than react. When we experience a roar, four outcomes can occur. We can succumb, survive, be resilient, or thrive in response to the roar. These outcomes are well demonstrated by Charles Carver.

Carver's Responses to Adversity

Charles Carver described four possible responses that humans portray when faced with a roar (an adverse event): succumbing, surviving, resilience, or thriving. Each is distinguishable and important to understand. Figure 2.1 illustrates the four levels of response.[8]

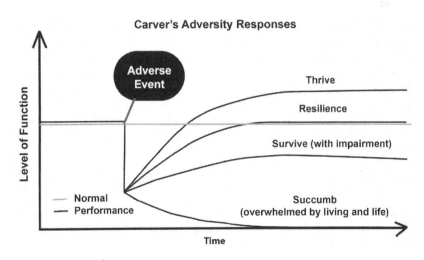

Figure 2.1 Carver's Adversity Responses
This diagram illustrates the four levels of functionality that can occur in response to adversity (crisis).

We will be referring to these four responses throughout this book. To be fair, each option has advantages and disadvantages. In our lives, each of us has chosen each of these four responses at least once, but some of us choose one or two more than others.

Sometimes it is easier to succumb or just survive. To succumb is to be unable to rebound from the adverse event, in other words, to be overwhelmed by life and living. If life continues after this response, it is a life worse than before the event and unlikely to improve unless one starts to believe they can change their situation.

The next response, surviving (often with an impairment of some kind, whether it be emotional, physical, relational, psychological, etc.) also results in a life that is below but closer to what it was before and higher functioning than succumbing. After the adversity, these people are not able to bounce back to what they were before the event. Their destiny is now below their previous normal level; if they develop a positive and healthy mindset, they will be resilient and/or grow to thrive, but their immediate norm will be about surviving not resilience or thriving.

Resilience is sometimes confused with surviving but what's critical about resilience is that a person returns to their normal level of function while surviving is a state of subnormal functionality. When someone bounces back to the same level of functionality after adversity, they are resilient. Resilience does not always include growth.

Those that thrive use adversity to change something about themselves to become more functional than they were before. They adapt, learn, and grow out of the event and move forward at a higher level of functionality so that, when the next adversity hits, they are already better prepared than others and are better prepared to grow again from it.

Resilience

Resilience is the process of adapting well in the face of adversity, trauma, tragedy, threats, or significant sources of stress -- such as family and relationship problems, serious health problems, workplace stresses, and financial worry.

Resilience is not demonstrated when the going gets tough. It is not toughing it out or being strong and unaffected. Resilience is the ability to bounce back from adversity, take on difficult challenges and still find meaning in life, respond positively to difficult situations, rise above adversity, cope when things look bleak, tap into hope, transform unfavourable situations into wisdom, insight, and compassion, and endure.

Resilience refers to the ability of an individual, family, organization, or community to cope with adversity and adapt to challenges or change. It is an ongoing process that requires time and effort. People must take several steps to strengthen their ability to respond to challenges and not merely react.

The American Psychological Association says,

> *"Resilience is not a trait that people either have or do not have. It involves behaviors, thoughts, and actions that can be learned and developed in anyone."*[9]

In a sense, resilience is like a muscle. As challenges are increased and muscles are used, they grow stronger. If muscles are not used enough, they atrophy. Thus, like any physical training, resilience can be learned and become stronger. You might have been conditioned to respond to fear in a certain way, but this can be unconditioned with practice. We all have resilience some of the time, but we don't always transfer resilience from one situation to another.

Despite the energy required to remain resilient, research shows that resilience is ordinary, not extraordinary.[10] People commonly demonstrate resilience, but it doesn't mean that we have no difficulties, issues, or distress when we are resilient. Both resilience and thriving involve considerable emotional distress.

Resilience implies that after an event, a person or community can cope, recover, change, strengthen, or adapt to reflect different priorities that arise from the experience and prepare for the next stressful situation.

Resilience is the foundation for post-traumatic growth, which is the core of thriving. In other words, we cannot thrive if we have not learned to be resilient (just as we can't be resilient if we don't know how to survive). I am not pretending that it is easy.

Resilience is the most important defense people have against stress. It is important to build and foster resilience to be ready for future challenges. Resilience will enable the development of a reservoir of resources to draw upon during roars.

Thriving

If resilience means bouncing back from adversity, thriving means doing better after than before the adversity. So, to thrive means to grow, develop, or improve because of one's response to a roar rather than to be resilient.

Many have used words other than thrive to name the same or a similar concept, like flourish or prosper. Whatever one chooses to call this concept, the result must be more than rebounding to what was before, more than resilience. In this book, we use thriving.

Thriving is my choice because thrive means to grow vigorously and maintain the growth over time despite or because of surrounding conditions, while flourish, prosper, and succeed are more time-dependent (an end to the state tends to be expected) and conditions are not part of the definition. Prosper refers mainly to monetary gain; success means attaining something but not necessarily growing in the process; and, flourishing only happens when conditions are favourable.

Webster's Revised Unabridged Dictionary defines *thrive* as:

> "to grow vigorously: flourish; to gain in wealth or possessions: prosper; to progress toward or realize a goal despite or because of circumstances."[11]

Since I find context is always vital for meaning, let's look at the etymology of thrive. It comes from a Scandinavian source akin to Old

Norse *þrifask* "to thrive," originally "grasp to oneself," probably reflexive of *þrifa* "to clutch, grasp, grip, take hold of...."[12]

Peter Drucker, in his book *Managing Oneself*, uses the term *excellence* instead of thriving, but his definition is synonymous with our thriving, and states, "success in the knowledge economy comes to those who know themselves – their strengths, their values, and how they best perform."[13]

To translate this to thriving, we must know not only what our passion is but also our abilities, nature (personality), and life lessons. These are commonly called strengths and we must use them to thrive.

Often, people try to strengthen their weaknesses. Please do not do this; our weaknesses will always be weaker than our strengths are strong. We must use our strengths and find someone else whose strengths buffer our weaknesses.

A friend of mine was very proficient using Excel software. As I was struggling through my third spreadsheet software course, she informed me that she did not take software courses (I did not get it even after the first two I had taken!). What did I learn? It was quicker for me to email the information and the formulas I needed to use and ask her to put them into an Excel spreadsheet than it was for me to learn to do it on my own.

We should work on improving our strengths and know our weaknesses but do not waste time trying to improve weaknesses; this can lead to a myopic life that distracts us from our focus. Rely on others who are strong in our weak areas to do what we cannot.

Run Toward the Roar (RTTR)

The Run Toward the Roar approach to life acts like corrective lenses; it corrects our myopic reactions and lifts our heads and hearts to see a thriving future. I want to honor you, however: If you do not want to address myopic living, if you do not want to think about bigger things than the everyday issues you already deal with, then please pass this book on to someone else. You cannot get anywhere new by doing the same things over and over. I will introduce you to a mindset- (or ethos-) based approach to roars that rejects living a life of resilience and chooses to, instead, lift our heads and start honoring our values and destiny by thriving rather than merely surviving or staying resilient.

Many say, what's wrong with resilience? Nothing is, as I've already said, there are advantages and disadvantages to each response. But if you plan on resilience, don't fall into the trap of thinking that if you are resilient once, you will be forever – that's a little myopic. One tends to stop looking at the compass and their destiny when living in resilience. It's good to bounce-back and continue functioning, but anything that is not growing or becoming stronger is already starting to die. Resilience does not focus enough on the destiny and does not use the compass to its full potential – again, it's a little myopic.

Nearsighted people get caught thinking that a person can drift into success. They live life with their head down keeping busy with daily, minor crises yet think they are going to end up reaching their destiny without looking at the compass or out to their destiny. They haven't acknowledged that there is more than luck involved in success – there is inquiry, learning, growth, and work involved in success. The RTTR approach to life is the only one that addresses and conquers fears to allow us to travel down life's river with our heads up, looking forward, as we lean on our compass and keep an eye on our destiny.

The theme of this approach is from an old teaching which was described this way:

> *This old teaching story comes from the great African savannahs where life pours forth in the form of teeming, feeding herds. As the herds eat their way across the plains, lions wait in the tall grass nearby, anticipating the chance to prey upon the grazing animals. In preparation, they send the oldest and weakest members of the pride away from the rest of the hunting pack. Having lost much of their strength and most of their teeth, the roar of the old ones is far greater than their ability to bite.*

The old lions go off and settle in the grass directly across from where the strong and hungry lions wait and watch. As the herd enters the area between the hunting pack and the old lions, the old ones roar mightily. At the sound of the roaring, most of the herd panics. Blinded by fear, they turn and flee from the seeming source of danger. As they rush wildly in the opposite direction, they run right to where the strongest lions wait in the tall grass for dinner to arrive.[14]

Instead of running away from the roar and into the hunting party, Run Toward the Roar. To have any value, this must be an ethos -- or a mindset – it must become part of our character.

I am approaching this less as a program or a course, and more as a reframing of our thinking and mindset. I intend to present things that science is finding work in life. I am going to do this in a very pertinent, rather than theoretical, way.

Some Anchor Points

Before starting to build a RTTR ethos with you, I want to share some of the core anchor points around which we will pivot. We know that communication is never just what is said, it is what is heard. To ensure we are speaking the same language, I want to set some definitions. I want your new ethos to be something that energizes and strengthens you yet is not so challenging to talk about that it drains the motivation out of you. I call this communication drift.

Communication drift is subtle and -- if we are not diligent about checking-in with those with whom we are communicating – it happens without our noticing. Drift worsens when combined with becoming distanced from our values and goals -- if we lose sight of our compass and our destiny. We drift off-course only one degree at a time but, although not sudden, we often don't notice till it feels like we are almost 180 degrees from the direction we wanted to be moving, and then a roar happens and everything that was beneath the surface gets revealed.

I was talking with a client (now a friend) as he was going through some work and personal challenges. The work was exceptionally frustrating because everything seemed to be getting tied up in the processing, which was not well defined, and he was never allowed to talk to the customer after the sale to solve their concerns and make sure the work got done. Those in processing told the clients, "That's not what we do here..." but did not tell them (or my friend) how things were done. The result was that it started to reflect badly on my friend's credibility as customers came back to him and questioned what he'd sold them.

At the same time, he felt like his joy of working was fading. It was exhausting him as he wasn't sure where he was going or why. After talking through some things together, he realized that not only was he now facing a direction that he didn't want to go but, worse, he wasn't even sure how he ended up going that way. Everyone was using all the right words and terms – even the business acumen was correct -- but it was not coming across very well, so he had drifted from his course. The result? There was not much thriving happening in his work life.

We determined that his values were no longer being encouraged. As a result, he was taking less responsibility or initiative, and was only surviving rather than thriving as he once did. He still had some resilience but was not thriving.

I do not believe that anyone plans to drift off course. I have never met someone who planned to end up in an unhealthy situation. Yet, when we do not focus on our destiny, rely on the compass, and check on our communications, we can so easily get caught in a lifestyle that is a long way from thriving

The terms that follow are referenced and expanded as we grow forward in this book, therefore – to avoid communication drift – I describe them here so we are all on the same map as we move forward to thrive.

Ethos

The Merriam-Webster dictionary defines *ethos* as "the distinguishing character, sentiment, moral nature, or guiding beliefs of a person, group, or institution."[15] As originally used by Aristotle, it referred to a person's character or personality, especially in its balance between passion and caution.[16] As such, our ethos is never something that is decided once and not revisited; it is lived day-in and day-out.

We will spend the rest of our lives defining and refining our ethos. And that is ok! I would suggest it is critical to living a fulfilling life, whether you never move from the home you were born in or travel every country of the world.

Many of us know times when we have achieved freedom from something we thought was ruining our lives -- bad relationships, toxic workplaces, financial insecurity, physical, psychological, or emotional abuse in our homes -- yet we still feel trapped in some way. If we still feel trapped, we spend too much time looking backward (not watching our compass), feeling bitter and angry (not setting new goals or losing sight of our destiny), or choosing to live myopically (bouncing back and forth between our fears now that things have changed). We are thrown into these behaviors when we have not fully processed our feelings about the thing that we feel ruined our lives. Getting rid of the thing itself does not get rid of our feelings about it.

In essence, we must examine our feelings around the event or thing that caused pain and insecurity for us. We must acknowledge our feelings, understand them, grieve for ourselves, and love ourselves (stop feeling unhealthy shame or guilt) to overcome these adverse events.

Our ethos can help us do just that. If we choose to live with an open mind, particularly when it comes to our behaviors and why they happen, we can change and grow. If we choose to have an open mind about others, we will ask rather than assume their motives for behaviors.

Our ethos is the harness we learned to lean into in Chapter One; it's the compass guiding us along the river of life because it embodies our values and beliefs. It is critical to RTTR. We will spend most of our time in this book understanding, defining, and refining your personal ethos so we are prepared for roars as we move toward our destiny and lead others through crises, as well.

Passion

The term *passion* has become a term so overused that it's lost much of its power. It is now understood to be an emotional state or a measure of emotional intensity.

The oldest meaning of passion is "suffering, to endure."[17] The term was often used for martyrs who had to suffer severe emotional and/or physical trauma, torture, and/or public disgrace for their beliefs. Aristotle used the Greek form of suffering and experience, or pathos (emotional arguments), along with ethos[18] (ethical arguments) and logos (logical arguments)[19] to demonstrate the three modes of persuasion used to convince audiences.

Passion today can sometimes mean something that takes over ethos (character) and logos (the mind) to become one's *raison d'etre* or an obsession that allows one to do or focus on nothing else. Thriving requires passion, but for our purposes, it is not an obsession, but an intense, driving feeling or conviction. It is not overtaking ethos and logos but works as the driving force behind our character and our logic to lead to our destiny. Passion is the fuel for our growth and faithfulness.

Passion is the fire in the bones about something or someone that we care deeply about. It is that sense of wanting something so badly it hurts. It is *passion fidelis*; not the drudgery of a slave's faithfulness [obedience] or the emotional whimsical passion of a teenager's first love.

Courage

Courage comes from the word for heart in Old French [corage] and Latin [cor]. Courage refers not to the physical heart but to the base of your ethos and your passion, your will. It is the inner strength beneath your ethos and passion and involves conviction, resolve, and commitment; it ensures your faithfulness and loyalty to RTTR.

Crisis

From the Greek *krisis*, which means *testing time* or *a contest*. I will reference crisis a lot, and I may spell it with a *c* or a *k* because I think the word crisis has been given a bad reputation. Krisis means decision,[20] not merely a catastrophe or chaos. And what is wrong with making a decision? Life consists of challenging times – both small and big – every day that require decisions.

Krisis has some amazing defining characteristics. The first three are somewhat obvious and would fit into our usage of crisis today. These are that the event is unexpected, it creates uncertainty, and it is seen as a threat to important goals. Nothing new there, right? It is the last characteristic of Krisis that is different. Krisis *requires change*.

I love the way S.J. Venette argues this point "...crisis is a process of transformation where the old system can no longer be maintained."[21] He later adds, "...if change is not needed, the event could more accurately be described as a failure."[22]

I know some motivational speakers have said that the Chinese word for "crisis" is made up of the symbols for opportunity and danger but, when this origin is checked by linguistics, it is false. It is not simply luck and courage that gets people through a crisis successfully. We need to be clear in our response because we need courage, passion, and ethos to be able to thrive.

Faith

Many get hooked by the term or concept of faithfulness because of its association with and use by religions. It has also been used to describe whether or not partners in a marriage have sexual relations with only one another. The meaning of faithful is to remain loyal or steadfast or true to the facts or the original.

As mentioned, the US Marines have a motto – *Semper Fidelis* – which in Latin means, *always* (semper) *faithful* or *loyal* (fidelis).

It is this variation of faithful that is used in this book. The idea that you are *Semper Fidelis*, or unwaveringly committed, to your values, your ethos, your passion, and your goals or destiny, not your fears. For our purposes, the *passio fidelis* as previously mentioned.

To thrive, to be fulfilled, we must decide what or who to be faithful to or trust. No decision is just a decision. Krisis will always reveal the results. Rely on your values (compass), goals (destiny), pathos (passion), and ethos (mindset), combined with courage, to make you take the RTTR approach to daily life.

Refinable New Norm

We have mentioned that our primitive reactions to a roar are a normal way to react to something abnormal. But usually, during a crisis, the abnormal conditions result in a new normal. A recent example of shifting to a new normal is the world's reaction to COVID-19. As a new norm occurs or is forced upon us, we must adapt and adjust to the new norm.

When I started crisis management work, I taught people to define their new norm. But I soon realized that any new norm is not a static concept determined at one point in time but a constantly growing concept as we face new challenges every day. I immediately started using the term *refinable new norm*.

To understand a refinable new norm, we must look at the definition of refine, which is:

- To reduce to a pure state; purify.

- To remove by purifying.

- To free from coarse, unsuitable, or immoral characteristics.[23]

Refining has long been used in Metallurgy, in which ores go through many processes to extract the purest metal possible. Via those processes, metals are refinable. Similarly, our new norm is refinable as each roar provides the opportunity to refine it into a new norm. Our normal is never just that, it is always new and it is always refinable; it is always a *refinable new norm*.

A refinable new norm allows three things to occur:

- As we experience roars and run toward them, we purify our values and destiny. The RTTR approach encourages unimportant things to get burned away and important things to remain, so we change, grow, and thrive.

- As we become nearer to our destiny, our focus becomes clearer.

- Everyone defines and refines her/his *own* refinable new norm.

This definition of each individual refinable new norm is determined by a simple formula:

The Refinable New Norm [Defined] = A + B + C, where

A = Attitude

B = Beliefs

C = Connections

This is core to the RTTR approach, and we will be looking at these concepts in more detail soon.

Setting Goals And Definitions

Developing and maintaining a RTTR Ethos involves refining, defining, and goal setting. Not once but throughout our life as we travel down the river and hit roars, buoys, and hazards that threaten to throw us off course. To simplify the processes of goal setting we will use the concepts of SMART goal setting and for definitions, we'll use the PIES formula.

SMART Goal Setting

Many of us have heard the term and worked with the concept of setting SMART goals, an idea which was first introduced in 1968 by Edward Locke but didn't gain wide recognition until November 1981 when it was summarized by George T. Doran in an article in *Management Review*.[24]

Originally applied for setting management and business goals, today SMART goal setting is used in all areas of life, including RTTR.

The acronym SMART represents the qualities that every goal should include:

Specific

The goal should be well-defined and specific, otherwise, it is tough to focus or feel motivated to achieve it. People suggest answering the five W questions:

- **What** do I want to accomplish?

- **Why** is this goal important for me?

- **Who** is involved?

- **Where** is it located?

- **Which** resources or limits (e.g., time, talents, skills, etc.) are involved?

Example: I will lose 10 pounds vs I want to lose weight

Measurable

There must be some way to measure progress. When we can measure our progress and completion, we are motivated to press on as we start to see the goal get closer. Because it is a measurement, numbers are often involved.

Questions that need to be answered are things like:

- How will I know when it is accomplished (I.e., how much, how many)?

- Are there indicators that can be used to measure progress (i.e., milestones to meet along the way)?

Example: I will lose 2.5 pounds a week till I lose 10 pounds vs I want to lose 10 pounds.

Achievable

The goal must be realistic and attainable; it needs to challenge and stretch your abilities but remain possible. An achievable goal will usually answer questions such as:

- How can I accomplish this goal?

- How realistic is the goal, based on other constraints (e.g., family commitments, job expectations, financial factors, etc.)?

Example: *I will lose 2.5 pounds a week to lose 10 pounds in 4 weeks* vs *I want to lose 50 pounds in 4 weeks.*

Relevant

The goal must be something of value and align with other goals. We must ensure the goal does not cost you achieving other goals or – if it does – you must be ok with sacrificing the other goal.

For goals to be relevant, the answer to each of the following questions should be *yes*:

- Is this something of value?

- Is now the best time?

- Does this match my other goals?

- Am I the right person to reach this goal?

- Is it applicable in the current socio-economic environment?

Example: *I will lose 2.5 pounds per week for four weeks to lose 10 pounds total by walking 10 miles a day so I'm healthy for my sister's wedding* vs *I want to lose 10 pounds in four weeks.*

Timely

We need to set deadlines for milestones of progress and completion of goals. The deadlines help us focus and keep working. This is important when setting more than one goal or adding a goal to others we have already set. If we have used the first four SMART steps, when timing conflicts arise, we will know which has more priority than the others.

A timely goal will usually answer these questions:

- When will I complete this goal and by when will I complete it?

- What can I do five days from now?

- What can I do five weeks from now?

- What can I do today?

Example: *I am going to lose weight by walking from 7:30-9:00 AM on Monday, Wednesday, and Friday mornings. I will walk on Tuesday and Thursday evenings between 6:45 – 8:15. I will be walking on either Saturday or Sunday morning from 9:00 -10:30 and take the other day off versus I want to lose 10 pounds in 4 weeks so I'm healthy for my sister's wedding.*

The PIES Formula

Thriving requires us to work at reframing our life. When refining, defining, or re-defining anything in your RTTR ethos, it is imperative to follow the PIES formula:

Positive

Frame your definitions positively rather than negatively. This is harder than it sounds because it is much easier to say what we don't like rather than what we do. For example, if defining a new norm, people are quick to say: *I don't want negative people in my life*, which is a negative statement. Instead, state it in positivity: *I will surround myself with positive people.*

And remember to use SMART goal setting (discussed above) when forming any definition. The statement I don't want negative people in my life still needs to be made Specific, Measurable, Achievable, and Relevant.

In Your Control

The important thing here is to determine what you *can* control and what you *cannot* control – whether it is situations, people or something else. The only person *you* can change, or control, is you. You cannot force a person to respect you, you can only control or change how you interact with (and respect) that person so they may respect you. And, again, the principles of SMART goal setting must be applied.

For example: If you want your child to respect you more, the statement *I want her/him to respect me more* is not something you can control. You must determine what respect means to you using SMART.

If respect for you means people are willing to hear your thoughts and feelings, it starts by modeling it with others. Thus, applying SMART goal setting, the statement above becomes something like *I will listen to my son every day to improve our communications and reflect his thoughts and feelings to him; I will show him respect and ensure understanding of what he is saying and meaning. I will follow up with him every four weeks to see if I have improved, or more growth is required. I will continue to model the respect I want to earn from him.*

Environment

How will your environment affect or be affected by this new definition? Will you need to move into a new environment? How will that affect you? How will it affect your old environment? And do you need to worry about that?

An addict often must change her/his environment to stop her/his addictive behavior. This may be frightening for her/him, others may resist the change, and both the addict and others in the old environment may suffer losses (of relationships, home, money, etc.) when the addict moves or stops seeing them.

Again, when defining Environment, application of the SMART principles must occur.

Example: *I will go to a parenting class in the evenings once a week for four weeks to learn how to listen to my son without judgment. As I begin to change my communication style, I will change the home environment by ensuring my technology is off so that I listen and understand, and the environment is changed to support this positive goal. This may confuse, anger, or relieve my son. I do not know the outcome for him, but I will be committed to implement and practice the communication skills I learn in the class while reminding him I want to have a positive relationship with respect.*

SMART

Be sure you remember that every step of PIES must be SMART. This is the final step of the process – be sure to look at your definition, when you think it is complete, to ensure that it meets all the qualities of SMART goal setting: Specific, Measurable, Achievable, Relevant, and Timely.

Hope And Faith

Faith encompasses one's current belief system, which may include life lesson experiences sourced from our exploration of external truths or other quests. Hope, on the other hand, is a desire deep in one's soul for something to happen in the future. Faith is a conviction that something will happen; hope is anticipation that something will happen. The author of Hebrews shares a perfect iteration of the relationship between faith and hope, "Now faith is the assurance of things hoped for, the conviction of things not seen."[25] In faith, the evidence of one's conviction is so certain that it becomes a truth we can be anchored to.

Hope and faith are related to one another but not always related to thriving. What does connect directly with thriving is the hope rooted in faith. The principle provides clarity to live in faith while facing roars.

For us to thrive there must be hope beyond the current circumstances, and the faith to live it. We start with our values to build a passion that forms our faith that, when roars happen, we will have hope we will get through them. The great French high-wire aerialist Charles Blondin crossed a quarter-mile tight-rope stretched across Niagara Falls, between the United States and Canada, many times in 1859. There were huge audiences on both sides of the Falls to watch. He travelled back-and-forth many times by foot, on stilts, in a sack, and pushing a wheelbarrow. After one crossing of the rope, he asked the huge audience if they thought he could cross with someone in the wheelbarrow. The crowd responded with a resounding, "Yes!"

However, when he asked for a volunteer to ride in the wheelbarrow, no one uttered a sound. The audience had hope he would make all his crossings, but they didn't have faith in him. He had faith in himself – enough faith that he was willing to risk another's life (to him it wasn't a risk). This is the difference between hope and faith. Hope stands close by on the shore watching the crossing and wanting the best; faith is the willingness to sit in the wheelbarrow for the trip!

To define a refinable norm, we must find the faith that impels us to sit in our new norm while we grow forward despite the roars. We must have faith to create purposeful thriving. There also needs to be hope that the outcome will be a success.

Why does this matter? There is no doubt that hope and faith are very intertwined; we cannot have hope without faith and, to thrive, there must be hope beyond the current circumstances. I'm not a poet, of any form, but thriving is best summarized in the oft-quoted line from Andrea del Sarto, by Robert Browning, "Ah, but a man's reach should exceed his grasp, or what's a heaven for?"[26] If there is nothing to strive for, to press on toward, then thriving is an illusion – and I do not believe that.

To have a refinable new norm built on our convictions, regardless of what or how others may agree or disagree with us, is vital for our mental health and thriving. In essence, what I am suggesting here is a way of living, not a program to follow. So, there is no checklist to follow when we feel like we are capsizing, to move from staying mast up (resilience) to moving forward (thriving), there is only the faith to deal with the situation and our hope that the outcome, although different, will be successful.

Success And Work

I challenge you to reframe and rethink your definitions of *success* and *work* in order to thrive.

The common definition of success today is a *positive outcome*, whereas in the mid-1800s it was simply an outcome (positive, negative, or neutral). Originally, *success* came from the Latin *succedere*, meaning *to go under* from the root words *sub* (meaning *under*) and *cedere* (meaning, *to go*). Oddly, then, *success* is tied to being a follower. Thus, we have terms like "successor to the throne" or "successive integers." When we reframe our understanding of success to include the original meaning of the word, *success* is the outcome when we are faithful or loyal to our values despite the challenges, hazards, and hindrances we face.

Thus, the current, common understanding of success being defined by how many toys, how much money, how much power, or how much fame one has is immaterial. It is a simple truth that hearses do not have luggage racks. This definition also gives birth to the idea where there is a Will, there's relatives!

> *We must resolve to follow our values despite the roars that we hear.*

To thrive, to be more than resilient, means that we choose to be faithful and loyal to a value or conviction that requires consistent determination.

I dare you to measure success not in terms of outcomes such as increased power, prestige, or possessions, but whether you followed your values despite the roars in your way. Are you still on your course or do you need to refine it to follow your compass? Make success less about the outcomes and more about living your calling, your purpose in life, your destiny, which is thriving.

For the purposes of RTTR and thriving, it is important to recognize that each time you stick to your values, your ethos, is a success. For, regardless of the result, you are successful in going through life and crises by sticking to your values – your RTTR ethos.

If we say we are committed to something, but we do not work at that commitment, will we move forward? If it does not change who we are, is faithfulness involved? Whether it's a relationship, work, sports, or anything else, can there be true faithfulness and hope if there is no willingness to do the work that needs to be done to reach our destiny? I believe the answer to all three questions is, "No."

> *"The truth of the matter is that you always know the right thing to do. The hard part is doing it."*
>
> *-Norman Schwarzkopf, Jr.*

Doing the right thing is not easy, however the joy and contentment we feel when we are able to say, live, think, and know we did the right thing according to our values, are immense. Your faithfulness will attract those with similar values, even if they do not agree with everything you say. Great leaders and influencers are never loved by everyone, but they are trusted, respected, and imitated because they RTTR.

Let's look at this in the one area many of us must deal with: Work. Is work a curse for you? It is not for me. For many, success at work is reaching retirement age, so they can do what they like. If the goal in retiring is to do something else of value, that is one thing; but if work is something we only suffer until we can quit and start doing something we want to do, where is the thriving in that?

To thrive, we must be faithful and loyal to something that we are passionate about but it isn't easy to achieve all the time. Thriving involves effort, work, or – that other four-letter word – discipline.

Is there any one of us who has never done something wrong, dangerous, or downright stupid? Let me be clear: Thriving is never about doing something correctly or being perfect. To thrive and never trip or stumble is incongruous. We must fail or botch things up; if pride or perfectionism creates a fear of failure, it is impossible to thrive. If we do not stumble or err, resilience may be possible but – more likely – we will merely survive or succumb to the roars. I propose that there is little potential to thrive if there can be no failure. If we don't take risks, if our pride and/or fears of what might happen stop us, something worse has already happened. We did not try.

Think of the people we most admire, are they the ones who never did anything, never attempted anything, never risked anything? I love what Theodore Roosevelt said in 1910:

> It is not the critic who counts; not the man who points out how the strong man stumbles, or where the doer of deeds could have done them better. The credit belongs to the man who is actually in the arena, whose face is marred by dust and sweat and blood; who strives valiantly; who errs, who comes short again and again, because there is no effort without error and shortcoming; but who does actually strive to do the deeds; who knows great enthusiasms, the great devotions; who spends himself in a worthy cause; who at the best knows in the end the triumph of high achievement, and who at the worst, if he fails, at least fails while daring greatly, so that his place shall never be with those cold and timid souls who neither know victory nor defeat.[27]

I believe success and work are less about positive outcomes (increased power, possessions, or prestige) and more about how well we stay our course. It is about defining our destiny, based on values we each set individually. Thriving is about standing through all roars for someone or something.

A value might change its description over time, but its intent is consistent. For example, the core value of *family* is different as a young parent than as a grandparent, but both will require work, perhaps sacrifice, and faithfulness to be successful.

Teamwork

Life is a team sport. We are social beasts and desire to interact with others. This is one of the significant issues of the pandemic and mental health.

Even those who prefer to work alone must have some interactions with others to be fulfilled. If relying on others is a fear, it is one of the first roars you and I will face and we may face it often, but you are sure to have more success when you have a team than if you make a solo effort all the way along.

Who you select to be on your team and work with to reach a desired outcome is important. Whether it is friendship, co-workers, sub-ordinates, coaches, mentors, advisors, or peers, remember to fill different roles with different personality types. Many people are unsuccessful because of a very human tendency; they put people just like themself on their team. Each part of the human body has its own special function to maintain health. Just like the human body, your team cannot all be the same type of person and remain healthy.

Remember to choose some people who are transparent, or vulnerable, with you. Some of the people that have encouraged my greatest growth were quite annoying. And yes, they say the same about me! However, despite our differences, we work well by being frank and encouraging.

Prayer

Since I am pushing you to think about passion, faith, courage, crisis, krisis, ethos, and teamwork, I will mention one more, prayer. I'm not interested in discussing the concept of prayer, that is a personal choice, but I want to suggest a mindset prayer or motto for thriving. The easiest way to support a RTTR ethos, to ensure thriving, is to remember this simple, yet valuable, prayer (or re-word it into a motto):

> *God, grant me*
> *The serenity to accept the things I cannot change,*
> *The courage to change the things I can,*
> *And the wisdom to know the difference.*[28]

Whether you are religious or not, the truth in this prayer is what stands out and what we will be focussing on in this book.

CHAPTER THREE

Building Your RTTR Ethos

Are you willing to look at where your loyalties do (or don't) lie? This is critical to thriving rather than merely surviving or staying resilient: Identifying the values you'll stick to through thick and thin is vital. These values are the basis of your new ethos. It is challenging to develop a thriving ethos; you will have to work at it. It is not easy. But that's why I'm here, to encourage you along.

A Change in Thinking

If we do not change our thinking, we will continue to do the same things that are not working for us. I will challenge you to expand your thought processes and assumptions as we work through this book. This is very demanding work because we must observe our thoughts without criticism and only with openness. We must question what and how we think and determine why we hold those beliefs and our thought processes that lead us to those conclusions. For, to grow and thrive, we must challenge our thinking often, particularly in the beginning.

> *"We cannot solve our problems with the same thinking we used when we created them." -Albert Einstein*

Because we are what we think, if we have anxious thoughts, we'll be anxious people. We will always find what our mind is looking for. If

I expect people to dislike me, I will notice (and look for) people who dislike me. If I expect to be a person who thrives through roars, I will thrive through roars.

Our lives, attitudes, feelings, reactions, results, failures, successes, and personalities are formed by strands of thought that tie our brain cells together like a string of beads. If the strand is not strong enough, the beads become disconnected and scatter. When this happens, we must strengthen our thinking strands to collect all the pieces of our lives and string them back together again.

Solomon wrote, "Be careful how you think; your life is shaped by your thoughts."[29] Many, throughout time, have shared the same thing with different words. Marcus Aurelius said, "Your life is what your thoughts make it."[30] Descartes wrote, "I think, therefore I am."[31] The nineteenth-century Unitarian preacher William Channing wrote,

> *All that a man does outwardly is but the expression and completion of his inward thought. To work effectively he must think clearly. To act nobly he must think nobly.*[32]

Ralph Waldo Emerson summed it up nicely, saying, "A man is what he thinks about all day long."[33]

William James laid the foundation for today's motivational movement and positive-thinking literature with these simple words,

> *The greatest discovery of our generation is that human beings can alter their lives by altering their attitudes of mind. As you think, so shall you be.*[34]

As a very brief synopsis, there is Rational Emotive Behavior Therapy (REBT) developed from the work of psychiatrist Albert Ellis in the mid-1950s that is a form of cognitive-behavioral therapy.[35]

It is a short-term form of psychotherapy that helps to identify self-defeating thoughts and feelings, question the reasonableness of those feelings, and replace those unreasonable thoughts with stronger, more positive ones. Essentially, this approach helps people understand how unhealthy thinking and feelings create roars leading to reactions that inhibit a person's goals. REBT is about changing one's thinking using mental exercises. Is it really a shock that the focus of the mind tends to be where the feet travel?

I know that it sounds tiring, but life changes rarely come easily. Everyone wants the benefits of physical exercise without the effort, yet it is the effort that makes us feel so much better. It is the effort of changing our thinking that will ensure achieving our goals.

When we look back on change, we call it growth.

Consider testing or taking exams: Many of us get nervous before we have a test or exam, regardless of the type of test or the subject. We start getting nervous, we start thinking negatively, and we start feeling like the brain has gone offline so that when the test is before us, we question our ability to pass. The outcome is determined by our thinking: If we think we will fail, we will; if we think we'll pass, we'll pass. Of course, this must be predicated by the fact that we studied for the test!

The VERI Approach

The VERI approach develops our initiative so that we can build and strengthen our ethos. To anchor ourself to our core values, to those things we will be faithful to, regardless of the cost, is VERI simple – it's not easy, though! The VERI approach is more common sense than anything, but we know sense is not always common. Each step of the VERI practice depends on the preceding step and, this practice continues forever in the same way that growth is never a one-and-done practice.

- **Values** – we intentionally determine and define our Values and, in doing so, they become anchored in our core. These are defined so they can be described in behaviors.

- **Encourage** – once anchored, our Values can be Encouraged in everything we do as we start to think about them, start looking for ways to see them, and start to put people around us who will also encourage us to live by our Values.

- **Responsible** – when our Values are Encouraged, we become Responsible for our actions to live them.

- **Initiative** – when we are Responsible for our values, we take Initiative. It does not matter what it is in life, when something is of value most people will take the Initiative to act upon what is important (of value). Taking the Initiative is what thriving is all about. By taking Initiative, there may come those times when we may need to refine our values.

Instead of taking an accountability approach (looking at whether the result is positive or negative), which usually teaches people not to get caught doing the wrong thing more than doing the right thing, the VERI practice considers success as an outcome (taking and finishing an initiative) and not merely the result. This is especially true when it is not always something positive – because going through the VERI approach is success in itself.

Instead of thinking there is a checklist of performance measurements to achieve, we are anchored in our Values so they Encourage us (and others) to be Responsible and take Initiative. Following this process allows us to thrive!

By developing a VERI approach, thriving becomes possible as roars and hazards present themselves and we can trust our compass to get us through them. To move beyond succumb, survive, and resilience to thrive requires pressing on despite the hazards we must navigate. Therefore, we must be passionate about what we are doing. It requires that it be something of value and a passion for us.

This book and the RTTR Discovery Guide are proof that I'm still learning this. I've quit this project more times than I can count. All the fears, roaring waters, and hazards such as trusting the advice or guidance of the wrong people, strains on my relationships, struggles with writing, etc. have challenged me along the way. It is here that my faith and hope have connected and come into alignment.

I have been able to encourage people to discover their values and to be responsible for them; this has given me feelings of success as clients take the initiative. I want to admit that, yes, some of the results were not what we had hoped for, but the clients leaned forward and kept moving. The VERI approach has allowed me to honor my passion for helping and serving others. I can say that seeing people lean into their values has fueled my passion, which has propelled me along. I have been blessed by encouraging them. I received a note from a mom on this VERI theme. *"Our son would not be where he is today had it not been for you teaching us... encouraging us parents ... and that taking risks is ok (definitely not taught in my childhood). And now our son is in TV/New Media with the television industry and he's having a ball. ... I thank you and I thank God."*

Now, you must determine your VERI, which starts with determining your Values. Once you have determined your Values, the Encouragement, Responsibility, and Initiative steps follow. Part of determining our Values involves relationships within ourselves and with others. We must start with our inner relationships; we must be genuine with ourselves before we can be authentic with others. We must thrive within before we can thrive outside of ourselves. Thus, we must have a thriving relationship with our self before we can thrive with others.

Thriving Relationships

What is a thriving relationship? It is more than an intellectual pursuit. It is something that ripples out from the heart, soul, and mind because it is who we are. It manifests in actions, words, thoughts, emotions, morals, and beliefs because of a commitment to a RTTR ethos.

Let me expand this theme for a moment. If we look at relationships through a RTTR ethos, then we will be forced to ask ourselves some difficult questions. On one hand, there is an upside to lying to our *self*: It will create the illusion for us that we are doing OK, and everything is fine. On the other hand, I hope you don't have any hot water moments since what's inside will leak out and it might not be what you wanted. I call this the *'Hot-Water-Tea-Bag Principle'* – when we're put in hot water, what's inside will leak out.

Thriving requires using an inside-out approach. We will get revealed eventually, and when we are held up to the light and e-**value**-ated, we want our partner, kids, and friends to be the ones who say, without reservation, "Yes, that's exactly who s/he is/was, even during moments of intense association."

To get you thinking about this relationship theme, let me boil it down to some simple, yet difficult, questions:

- Will a relationship with the emotions/thoughts/people/morals/self-image get you where you want to go (this question implies you know where you want to go)?

- Will these relationships build me up or tear me down? Will they challenge me to raise the bar or to accept my situation as what it is?

Do you know the next part that happens if we want to have a thriving relationship? Not every relationship is good for us, the relationships that we have with some things will hinder us from thriving. For example, if I have a relationship with chocolate (and I do), it might hinder me from thriving physically. If I have a relationship with emotions in which I keep my feelings bottled up inside and tell everyone I am fine when I am not, I will not be able to thrive emotionally or communicate about my feelings.

Think about reframing wellness to think beyond a relationship as something between two or more people and consider the inner relationships with your *self* on such issues as emotions, spirituality, morals, and other character determiners.

To thrive, we must intentionally address our inner relationships. Whether we call it being genuine, being authentic, or having integrity, the state of being someone who relates to all our self allows us to have the faith to press on without fear. That is thriving and it starts with the relationship with our self.

I'm commending a VERI approach that resonates with your heart, soul, and mind to provide strength. We have decided to rely on our values during a crisis, so we can determine responses beforehand with training. Emergency workers are trained how to think, do, act, and even feel, during a crisis but training does not always engage their beliefs, heart, sense of faith, or spirit. The saving-lives-at-all-costs ethos takes time to develop (and some never do).

Those trained to respond while following an underlying ethos tend to be more prepared for crises – think of Marines and their *Semper Fidelis*; they are the most capable group of soldiers in the US Military. Once you determine your ethos and begin to respond rather than react to crises, you, too, will become extremely capable and resourceful when roars occur because your ethos will guide you more than anything else.

I wonder if people wrestle with the faithfulness theme in marriages because, so often, it gets defined inaccurately in two ways: first, it is defined as religious; and second, it is defined as what one is against rather than for.

To be fair, telling others what we do not like is easier than expressing what we do; many struggle with this. Being negative is a lazy approach to life and crises because it requires little effort, thinking, or commitment. Take note of the number of people who are more than willing to tell us what they do not like, what bothers them, what they do not find funny, etc. That is why social media can be so negative, users can sit and judge without all the information and with minimal effort.

If you have enough nerve or want to have some fun, turn the tables: Ask negative people what they do like. Ask them what they are for; what they do believe, what is it they want. Often, they get defensive as the hot water in which you've put them boils down to their thoughts, feelings, and beliefs and they will not know how or be able to answer.

Those who are motivated by their ethos may not agree with something or someone, but we do not get defensive. We can explain our rationale and what we believe. We may not agree with another's perspective, but we explain our position. That is the heart of thriving through krisis and transforming this into opportunity.

Let me explain using an adage from military personnel: *There are no atheists in foxholes*. When a person is feeling attacked, threatened, and fearful for their wellbeing or life, positive or hopeful thoughts don't usually come to mind first. A commitment to the faith that they *will* return home is required to survive.

In *Good to Great*, when author Jim Collins asked Vice-Admiral James Stockdale about the personal characteristics of prisoners who did not make it out of the prisons of war (POW) camps he said, "Oh, that's easy, the optimists".[36]

Not understanding this response, Collins asked Stockdale for clarification.

Stockdale replied, "Oh, they were the ones who said, 'We're going to be out by Christmas.' And Christmas would come, and Christmas would go. Then they'd say, 'We're going to be out by Easter.' And Easter would come, and Easter would go. And then Thanksgiving, and then it would be Christmas again. And they died of a broken heart."

After a silent pause, Stockdale added; "This is a very important lesson. You must never confuse faith that you will prevail in the end – which you can never afford to lose – with the discipline to confront the most brutal facts of your current reality, whatever they might be."[37]

This enigma became known as the Stockdale Paradox.

Faith is the heart, soul, mindset, and strength of thriving. You may not have your destiny fulfilled by Christmas, Easter, or Thanksgiving but there needs to be the commitment that, in the end, you will reach it.

Relational Resilience

What would happen if we tackled this by reframing the whole discussion? I'm suggesting that everything in life is about the relationship with something or someone. We have a relationship with the environment, our work, our colleagues at work, our neighbors, and this list can continue ad nauseam. If thriving is just a relational hypothesis, then crisis and change would be reframed into that moment when all the various elements converge at one time.

There is a story from the First World War about a deep friendship that formed between two soldiers in the trenches. These two buddies were serving together in the mud and misery of a European stalemate. Under fire, in the cold, in the rain, and under orders they lived their lives together.

The deadlock consisted of one side or the other arising out of their trenches and throwing their bodies at the opposing side's trenches for a time. Then they would drag themselves back to their trench, treat their wounds, bury their dead, defend their trench, and wait to do it all over again. Day and night through this horror they would talk to their trench mates about their families, their life back home, and their hopes and dreams for when they returned from their nightmarish existence.

On one charge, a soldier named Joe was severely wounded. His friend Gary made it back safely to the trenches while Joe lay suffering under the night flares, between the trenches, alone!

Danger kept escalating and between the trenches alone was no place to be. Gary wanted to go to his friend, to comfort him, to encourage him but the officer-in-charge refused to let Gary leave because it was too dangerous. When the officer turned his back, Gary went up over the side of the trench. Ignoring the blasts, the bullets, the gunpowder in the air, and his frantically beating heart, Gary made it to Joe.

Eventually, Gary pulled Joe back to the trench. It was too late, however, as his friend was gone. This officer, filled with a sense of I-told-you-so arrogance, saw Joe's body and said sarcastically, "Well, was it worth the risk?"

Gary responded immediately, "Yes, Sir. It was. Joe's last words made it more than worth it. Joe looked up at me and said, 'I knew you'd come.'"

This story shows that Gary had a strong relationship with himself, knew his values, and had relational resilience with his values as well as with his friend Joe, who would have done the same thing had Gary been left injured or dead between the trenches.

The VERI approach is always about taking initiative in relationships, with our self and others. To thrive and be more than just resilient requires us to define the values to which we will always be faithful or loyal. To go beyond resilience requires relational thriving. Rather than flying through life by the seat of our pants, let's take a sensible, practical, and relevant approach. Instead of dealing with our inner and outer relationships after the fact, let's instead make them something of value ahead of the roars.

Building Your VERI Community

Being willing to find people who will encourage you takes courage, but it is important to start building a community of support.

Supporters are not those shouting what we should do from the shores of the river, they are the people who are willing to get in the boat with us, even if the boat is sinking. They sit beside us and ask, "Do you want to talk to me? Or do you want me to paddle?" They play a variety of different roles depending on the situation we are in. They might be a mentor, a leader, a helper, a follower, a counselor, a colleague, or a friend.

I need you to think about this phrase: Blessed because we are inadequate.

It is something I seldom, if ever, hear people say and truly mean. Imagine our heart saying to our lungs, "I don't need you."

Or, our stomach saying the same thing to the intestine, or one part of our body saying it to any other part.

Yet, how many human health problems are rooted in that happening? When the white cells shut down, mutate, or go into overdrive, the pancreas or kidneys stop working or any number of things can go wrong and the whole body suffers.

Why is it that so many of us think we need to be and do everything on our own? Why do so many people work on being all that they can be without leveraging the strengths of others? A thriving community must consist of different people with different strengths. In the same way, the body can't only be one part to live, and a great sports team can't rely only on one player.

I suggest that we are fortunate because we are incapable of doing everything ourselves. To be blunt, are you able to connect and relate to people who see themselves as perfect and able to handle anything?

If we think of our VERI Community as a human body, and each person in the community as a body part, we must rely on and trust them to stay healthy. The others are the very components that make it all come together. The brain cannot thrive on its own, no more than the heart, lungs, or kidneys can. Why would anyone think that a person could thrive without the support and nurture of others? A single person might survive or be resilient, but they cannot thrive without others.

The members of your VERI Community will need to have different strengths than you. They should complement you even if they do not always compliment you. People who are very like me drive me nuts, but people who are very different than me can do the same thing. The key is the focus: What is the desired outcome of being together as a community?

Our VERI Community is where Values get to be Encouraged so that we are Responsible, which strengthens us to take the Initiative in the face of roars. That means common Values (on which everything is built) are more critical than any other characteristics of the community.

The key will be building a VERI Community that strengthens, nurtures, and reinforces what you are for (your Values). It encourages or challenges everyone in it to RTTR, even if someone wants to run in the opposite direction.

A healthy body, like healthy emotions, physical condition, thinking, morals, spirituality, and relationships, is challenging to maintain yet rewarding. Just like gardening, it requires cultivating, fertilizing, and pruning, but if it is left on its own it tends to just be weedy and overgrown.

Who are the people who have heard a roar and responded not reacted? Those are your people! You may want a mentor: Someone who will not tell you what to do but who models what to do for you and helps you learn to respond and thrive, so you do things differently next time. Over time, you will recognize these people more easily and they will recognize you, and you will become part of a community of helpers, teachers, and mentors who are value-anchored, have a RTTR ethos, and are committed to thriving.

The Importance of Planning

The road to success is dotted with many tempting parking places.

Unknown

All long and/or complicated journeys need to be guided by a plan: a strategy to follow that is adjusted and refined by the traveler as necessary (not a cut-and-paste copy of another's plan).

Have you ever noticed that some trips seem short? There are months of planning but – when you're on the trip – it seems like it just started when it ends? While a trip without a plan often results in regrets? I've realized this as a *learned* planner.

My approach, before meeting my wife, was to fly by the seat of my pants. Since I married – and proved opposites attract – my wife has demonstrated to me the plusses of planning. Before we take a trip, she studies things to see, places to go, and where to stay. The result is that the trip is amazing. We get to visit all the valuable stops, with my contribution of some spontaneous activities, and return home satisfied. My trips without a well-thought-out plan resulted in me arriving home to discover all the things I would have loved to have done or seen but missed.

In life, can we expect to grow and thrive without a plan? If we don't know what is important to see and do, where we are going (and where we have been), and who our traveling companions are, can we do any more than survive or be resilient?

That does not mean our plan cannot be interrupted or swayed by spontaneity, nor does it mean we don't come upon buoys (fears) or hazards that cause us to have to detour. But, having a plan allows us to stay on course, even if we want to change it.

Years ago, when farmers walked behind a horse and plow to till the soil, they often met boulders, stumps, stubborn horses wanting to eat or return to the barn, and other hazards that threatened the straightness of their rows, but they still managed to maintain straight rows. I have never worked behind this type of horse and plow, but I know how easy it would be to get a row that looked like a squiggly line or veered off at an angle. In a short distance, this is not vital however the longer the row the more important a straight line is.

How did the farmers maintain their path with all these obstacles in their path?

The farmer would tie a flag on a post at each end of the field marking the row they wanted to plow. The farmer would then steer toward that flag from the other end of the field. When the plow reached the flag, the flag would be moved over a distance so that the return trip would have a point to drive toward. The result is that – even when the farmer hit rocks, stumps, or other challenges in the field – the row did not go off course or stop, its progress was just delayed.

When we work through and overcome detours from the plan, we learn, and our confidence grows. Focussing on a flag or our destiny will result in thriving beyond resilience because we have a plan to achieve something of value. The relationships we have with a trusted VERI Community during these times will be lifesaving and become even more valuable as we travel along our route.

A VERI PLAN

To be able to refine new norms and RTTR, we must have a life purpose to support us and keep us leaning forward so that, when we do fall, we fall forward. This life purpose is our VERI PLAN.

I propose that to take the initiative to change or continue anything, the *anything* must be something of value. Remember that the I in VERI – Initiative – only exists if the first 3 letters are in place: Values, Encouragement, and Responsibility. If we don't value something, we will never be Encouraged or Responsible enough to take any Initiative.

In the early 2000s, I was involved in the downsizing of some hi-tech sector companies. I proposed, developed, and implemented this VERI PLAN approach to support these impacted personnel while on a contract with an outplacement agency working with the dramatic downsizing of some hi-tech companies. The impact on the individuals involved, their families, and the community was enormous and lasting. I was employed to help those being let go. In some ways, it was a very enjoyable role: I was there to help people define or refine what their values and plans would be moving forward.

The people I worked with told me that part of the feeling of loss, other than the job itself, was that they realized they had traded in at least some of their original passion for their profession for company priorities to keep their job. They had forgotten what their real passion was. When we were looking at finding their focus and clarifying their values, the first thing that we had to do was rekindle their passion.

They needed to take the time to refine and re-define what they loved about their work. We ran what we called "Information and Referral" meetings, in which they talked with and questioned people about how they got into their field, what they like about their field, and what they would change. Rather than scrambling to find a new job, focussing only on income – to keep providing for their family and themselves – these employees were allowed time to clarify what they were passionate about and then start making changes and moving onward – this became their VERI PLAN.

What Does PLAN Stand For?

PLAN is the key to building a life that thrives through roars.

While our VERI is a personal, internal determination, there are others with whom we have common values and, as a result, common VERIs and, thus, we do and should find and build a VERI Community to help support our destiny.

Our PLAN, on the other hand, is also personal and internal, but it is unique; no one PLAN is the same as another. Everybody's PLAN is singular because we all follow a different, individual path through life based on our personality, strengths, weaknesses, life lessons, environment(s), culture, experiences, and perceptions.

Passion

Our passions can be influenced by our Values, and subsequently, by our individual VERI (because we are always ready to take Initiative about our Passions). To reach the Initiative phase, we must have already attained the VER and Values are the beginning of everything.

Passion is not merely an emotion but something far deeper. Passion is that place in your heart, in your soul, where you care so deeply about something that it either brings tears to your eyes or anger to your spirit. Let me clarify that anger and tears are neither wrong nor right, it is what we cry and get angry over that encompasses our passions.

Passion can take the form of so many different expressions. It's been described as a fire in the bones or the gut. It may be held by an individual or a group of people, even an age demographic. It includes an issue, which can range from air quality to water conservation to the type of vehicle people drive to any number of things. I want to remind you that many people will rain on your parade if you share your passion with people who are not living theirs.

Your passion is part of what makes you unique and special and, therefore, to thrive and RTTR, it is vital to fan the flames of those fires within you. Passion feeds positive, forward growth.

Life Lessons

From the day we are born (and maybe before that) we start learning life lessons and everyone's lessons and learning are unique in content, timing, impact, effect, strength, culture, environment, and conditioning.

We all learned to talk but the timing and content of our first word, first phrase, and first sentence are all individual based on who has been talking to us, what we have heard, what is around us, what culture and environment we are in, and what we perceive as being important. All our life lessons are the same. From one event involving 30 people, 30 or more life lessons will evolve.

Ability

Our abilities also influence our path. We tend to use – unconsciously – those skills we are naturally good at. It's a survival technique of living organisms. Do what you are best at to survive and follow the path that allows you to use your strengths rather than your weaknesses to make life easier.

Nature

Our personality affects our passion, our life lessons, our abilities, and our perceptions. Our nature is how we are wired. It affects our values and our passions. Understanding our nature helps us PLAN around our values.

Our passions tell us where we are to serve and add value. Our nature is how we serve and add value. The irony is many times conflict happens around values and natures. Some people tend to be very task-oriented while others are more people-oriented, some like to be behind the scenes while others like to be very active and outgoing. Neither is good nor bad, they are simply different preferences.

If we do not have different natures around us, we will hinder ourselves because we do not see and think of what these people who are different than us can. They should be part of our VERI Community. Note that our nurture impacts how we understand our wiring. Therefore, our life lessons will and can impact our nature, which in turn affects our passions and abilities.

Knowing our passion, our life lessons, our abilities, and our nature are critical to knowing what path we need to follow – and each path will be as unique and varied as there are people on the earth.

Why A VERI PLAN Matters

The question that will kill anybody's passion quicker than anything is a very simple, well-intentioned one, "How are you going to make any money doing *that?*"

The number of people that I have met – especially young people – who have heard that question in one form or another is overwhelming.

There is a very simple principle at play here. If you do not know where you are at and you do not know where you are going, *how* is a completely irrelevant question. Therefore, asking anybody questions about employment, paying bills, or earning an income, when they are not clear on what their values and passion are, is irrelevant. And is, quite frankly, morally wrong.

I am sorry if this sounds harsh, but I am tired of people's plans being discouraged and discounted before they even get to start. I'm left with the question, "How can we expect a human being to be resilient, nevermind thrive, when we do not encourage them when they are getting started?"

Finally, society is realizing that it is always better to hire for values and passion than for skills. Many businesses and employers have discovered, the hard way, that if a candidate's employment is based solely on her/his skills, s/he will soon either burnout or focus on doing a bare minimum to hold-out for the benefits until they can take their pension. Many have also discovered that when they hire the shining star or the highest-skilled person, that person often runs into conflicting issues around working with others, teamwork, competition, culture, and values.

My assertion is simple: The best thing an employer or any organization can give their workers is a place to work their PLANs, which honors employees' values. Our worth cannot be defined by our paycheck or other benefits.

In a coaching call with a business owner recently, we talked about his success and future focus. As he talked about developing his business, and increasing his success and profit, I asked him what I thought was a practical question, 'Where do you go after that? If you create the big business and get the success you want, what happens next for you? There is only one direction to go from the top of the ladder...."

Our values must be in play for us to be able to thrive. Values are not ethics; they are those areas that motivate us. People are motivated by all sorts of different values and often more than one. It could be money, looks, relationships, integrity, credibility, family, etc. As we mature and grow, life is about discovering the values that matter to us as an individual so that we can serve ourselves and others in the VERI way that matters and lasts.

To illustrate this in two very different ways I share with you two funerals that I attended. One was a man who lived his entire life in a small town. He was a businessman who did tire sales with some automobile services. Over his 35 to 40 years of being in business, he had employed all sorts of different people and kids. He always took the time to do the extras, including helping anonymously. He died 30 years after he had been in business. When Alzheimer's disease finally took his life, his funeral was so crowded that some people had to stand and listen to the service from outside the hall where it was held.

At the second funeral, people talked about what a great member of the community the deceased was. They talked about all the things he had done, places he had been, and other things he was recognized for. The difference was that there were only six of us at the second funeral.

Neither of these funerals was better than the other – at both funerals, people had very good things to say about the deceased. They simply illustrate that one's values and PLAN determine the road that one takes. One man was passionate about relationships and helping others; the other was passionate about achievements rather than relationships. Both followed their passions.

Imagine traveling your river toward your destiny if your purpose is your VERI PLAN. Your potential is living that VERI PLAN whether you are in front of crowds of others or on your own. That sweet spot where life does not get better than this, or more exciting. Where, when you know things are not going well you also know you are growing forward. Remember, a trip should be about the adventure, not merely the destination. You are aimed in the right direction and focused. Whether we call it being genuine, authentic, or acting with integrity, the reality of being true to ourselves is that there is no fear because we have the faith to press on. That is thriving and it starts with the relationship with ourself.

· PART II ·

The ABCs

My grandma used to say, "The road to hell was paved with good intentions." We can be aimed in the right direction but an eddy, a crosswind, or many other roars will happen, so we need have more than good intentions.

I have seen many people struggle with programs, books, and courses designed to help participants thrive. For me, there is always a stumbling block: It is the nagging question, "Now what?"

Perhaps I need encouragement and someone who is willing to journey with me or perhaps it is my thinking style, but I want to know what the process is, what the steps will be, and what the program, book, or course will do to or for me before I commit to doing the work. I need to know the *how*, *why*, and *what* before I can put my shoulder into rowing.

That's what this section of **Run Toward the Roar** is about: *what* the core elements of resilience and thriving are (the ABCs); *why* the ABCs factor into our success; and, *how* to use the ABCs. Obviously, I'd be honored if you want me to journey with you, but the ABCs are what we will work on whether you work with me personally or use this book and the Discovery Guide as your support. Either way, you will be challenged.

The ABCs consist of three elements that are critical to RTTR: Attitudes, Beliefs, and Connections. Each element consists of two areas of resilience that are required to thrive:

- **Attitudes:** We will look at two components which significantly impact our attitude, the physical, (including some human chemicals, hormones, stress, grief, fear, and REST) and balancing feelings and emotions (which are not the same thing).

- **Beliefs:** We will look at the cognitive and mental elements of resilience (in other words, we'll be thinking about our thinking) and explore the spiritual – not religious – reality of thriving and resilience.

- **Connections:** We will explore two areas that are often challenging but must be resolved to be able to RTTR, relationships and morals.

Examining and understanding our ABCs will allow us to RTTR and thrive despite how others may think or feel. As the core of your being, your ABCs are as critical as your ethos and are couched within your faith, values, and behaviors. We will focus on transformation (forward growth) and strengthen your commitment to your values and destiny, so you thrive regardless of the roars that arise in your life.

Ironically, whether it is resilience or thriving you want, who you are is seldom reflected in the outcome; it is your focus and direction that reflects who you are and how you are known by others. When we are focused on our ethos, people may have observations or opinions, but if they are not helping us, we love them enough to say thank you and press on.

• CHAPTER FOUR •

A is for Attitude

A key theme we must start with is simple: *What's with the attitude?*

Our attitude shapes everything in our life: our decisions, relationships, career, emotions, health, values, our PLAN, etc. The fantastic thing is that you get to choose your attitude – how you view and approach every situation and challenge.

When a positive attitude that is anchored to a RTTR ethos is combined with faithfulness, values, courage, and dedication, amazing things can happen.

Our attitude is the lens through which we view life. We see everything through it, and it determines how well we face or bounce back from a roar. Our attitude affects our perception of a river hazard, it determines our thoughts about a hazard, from *I'm going to be ruined* to *I'm going to be damaged, but I can survive* to *I'm excited and I can't wait to brag about this one on the other side!* Because attitudes can change, you might even start with the first, move through the second (or stop at it), and – if you RTTR – settle on the third or a variation of it.

Thriving through a roar is key to navigating the river of life and reaching our destiny. Setbacks, challenges, and problems are inevitable, but our attitude toward roars determines how quickly we can transform the crisis into an opportunity. Changing our attitude helps change our response to roars.

Our attitude is made up of emotions, behaviors, and beliefs (which are based in upbringing, experiences, and memories), making it complicated to dissect and examine. For our purposes, we are going to look at how attitude, behaviors, emotions, and feelings interact to direct our lives. Along the way we will look at negative stress, grief, and fear.

Chuck Swindoll, founder of Insight for Living, said:

> *The longer I live, the more I realize the impact of attitude on life. Attitude, to me, is more important than facts. It is more important than the past, than education, than money, than circumstances, than failures, than successes, than what other people think, say, or do. It is more important than appearance, giftedness, or skill. It will make or break a company ... a church ... a home. The remarkable thing is we have a choice every day regarding the attitude we embrace for that day. We cannot change our past ... we cannot change the fact that people will act in a certain way. We cannot change the inevitable. The only thing we can do is play the one string we have, and that is our attitude ... I am convinced that life is 10% what happens to me and 90% how I react to it. And so it is with you ... we are in charge of our attitudes.[38]*

The Eddy Effect

Many of us become stuck in a rut or sucked into an eddy, repeating a pattern of behavior and results as we travel our river. It is similar to myopic thinking (Chapter One). I like to call this the Eddy Effect: we let our emotions dictate our behavior(s), which set our attitude, which affects our feelings. So often we let our negative feelings steer our behaviour which, in turn, turns our attitude to the negative, and that makes us feel even worse. We are drawn into an eddy of despair (see Figure 4.1).

A rut is just a grave with both ends knocked out.

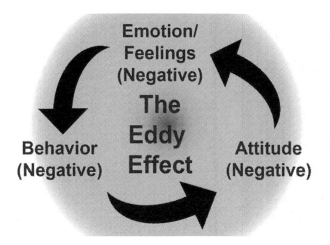

Figure 4.1. The Eddy Effect
During the Eddy Effect, our behavior and attitude are led by our emotions (which, during roars, can be fear based). Our emotional state causes us to behave in negative ways which tends to affect our attitude in a negative way. Our negative attitude affects our feelings negatively and we are pulled into a vicious eddy (whirlpool) that continues to pull us down and we fall into an eddy of despair.

When we are stuck in The Eddy Effect, we continue doing things that work against thriving. We behave unhealthily. Our emotions and feelings are steering us instead of our attitude. This becomes a weight that drags us down and affects what we will be faithful and loyal to. It's like trying to keep our bow above water while having too much cargo on board – we worry more about staying afloat than capsizing and aren't paying attention to where we are going (our destiny).

Think about dieting: When the attitude for the diet is *I'm doing this to lose weight*, the diet plan often feels like a punishment (I have to stop eating what I enjoy to lose weight). It's almost impossible to stay committed to a punishment. The Eddy Effect is in motion.

If we reframe our attitude for dieting to, *I'm doing this to live a long, healthy, fulfilling life*, the diet plan doesn't feel like punishment, it feels like a reward. Our new attitude makes changing our behaviors and emotions easier. Yes, it is still a struggle for many of us, however the focus is less on the *shoulds* and *should nots* and more on *I am going to....*

Everything can be taken from a man but one thing: The last of human freedoms – to choose one's attitude in any given set of circumstances, to choose one's way.[39]

The Bearing Solution

According to Hogg & Vaughan, an attitude is "a relatively enduring organization of beliefs, feelings, and behavioral tendencies toward socially significant objects, groups, events or symbols."[40] For our purposes, Paul words how a faithful attitude figures in RTTR perfectly:

> *No, dear brothers and sisters, I have not yet achieved it, but I focus on this one thing: Forgetting the past and looking forward to what lies ahead, I press on to reach the end of the race....*[41]

Starting with the commitment to be faithful, our RTTR attitude directs our physical and emotional states into alignment with it. This is the heart of a psychotherapeutic approach called Cognitive Behavioral Therapy (CBT). In short, CBT focuses on changing negative thought patterns to change behaviors and feelings. I incorporate CBT in what I call The Bearing Solution (see Figure 4.2). The Bearing Solution starts with changing an attitude by redefining it and basing it in values we are committed to, which then affects our behaviors, and our new behaviors improve our feelings. The positive feelings then reinforce our attitude.

Like The Eddy Effect, this is a cyclical sequence but – rather than dragging us down into ever-increasing negativity and despair – The Bearing Solution is a vortex that pulls us up out of negativity and despair and raises us up so we can see the horizon, our destiny, and continue to move toward it despite roars and fears along the way.

Figure 4.2. The Bearing Solution
The Bearing Solution starts with a positive attitude, which leads to positive behaviors that promote positive feelings that support our Attitude. Rather than spiraling downward in a negative spin, we spiral upward and outward, regaining our course and heading to our destiny.

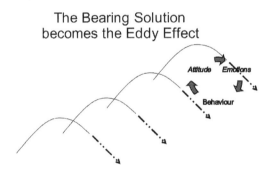

Figure 4.3. Be Cautious!
The Bearing Solution Can Become The Eddy Effect.
When our faithfulness is growing, we can grow to the next level. At any point we can pause, coast, or stop – or plateau. if this happens, our Bearing Solution falls into the Eddy Effect. We stop developing and fall into reacting rather than responding, once again.

Building A RTTR Attitude

The first step, once we choose to adopt a RTTR attitude, is to determine what values matter to us and to which we are faithful (our RTTR ethos, Chapter Three). Then, we must build an attitude committed to that ethos. We must put The Bearing Solution into play.

The struggle in this process comes with the decision to change our attitude – we usually develop our initial attitudes without thinking about it. We simply react to the things that happen to us when we are young, accept them, and form our attitude. But we can make a conscious effort to change acquired attitudes – to do so, we must *choose* and *commit* to the change. Complacency in our acquired attitude will not take us to where we want to go.

It is the decision to change what our *enduring organization of beliefs, feelings, and behaviors* will be when we face roars that starts to change our attitude. To live authentically, we must, at some point, have the discipline to choose for ourself. There will be times when we do not want to press on, to persevere, when we want to just drift. At these times, we risk getting caught in The Eddy Effect.

For example, exercising. Sometimes we know we should do some exercise, but do not feel like it. If we do nothing (follow our feelings – The Eddy Effect) we feel bad (physically and/or psychologically). However, when we do the exercise, despite how we feel beforehand, we always feel better for doing it, both physically and emotionally.

I was working with a business owner who'd bought a new business. He had 'inherited' some personnel with approaches that were significant barriers to growth and customer service, not to mention a healthy team-work environment.

While the new owner hated conflict, we clarified the values and the focus so that as the process unfolded, the flashpoints became self-evident. He needed to act on something that had been going on for a few years, and when he spoke with the person to walk through an exit strategy for them, he couldn't believe how, within one hour, the weight that was off his shoulders. It actually felt like he could get a deep breath when he thought about his work.

Our attitude determines how we behave toward events, people, and things, and characterizes us. For example, if our *enduring organization of emotions* is to show no emotions or to show all our emotions *toward socially significant objects, groups, events or symbols*, our behavior becomes a reflection of one of two extremes and reveals who we are. The attitude characterizes us: in the first case, others see us as a cold, uncaring, selfish person and, in the second, they see a weak, overwhelmed, and dramatic person.

Knowing our ethos and clarifying our attitude help predict the behaviors we demonstrate and give us a sense of control. Our new attitude helps us through experiences so – even if we have no control over the event or the outcome – we can choose how we respond to whatever is happening. We demonstrate who we are, not what has happened to us.

Always Keep Steering

When life seems to be going as planned, it's comfortable and mostly predictable. That's where most of us prefer to stay. I don't want to fearmonger, but we do not know what is around the corner. Be it a health concern, loss of a significant relationship, or a massive change, there is some crisis coming that will knock us out of our comfort zone, no matter what.

Floating along a gently rolling river, our boat seems to be calmly moving forward. We don't even have to steer, and we can get lulled to sleep, drifting off, feeling secure. But just because we are moving doesn't mean we will end up where we want to go!

Just because we are moving doesn't mean we will end up where we want to go!

Steering the boat is active work. In the long run, the passive approach of floating or drifting doesn't work. If we are not paying attention, watching our compass, and trimming our course, it is highly unlikely our boat will end up where we intend. At some point, we end up in treacherous waters with the rapids tossing us around among jagged rocks and other unseen hazards beneath the surface. Things that have become part of our journey because we are off course

Just like any river, life will have bumps and knocks that create dents and holes in the boat or capsize us. Although we can relax somewhat during calm times, we must always remain aware of our progress and direction – we must keep track of our bearing.

It's our attitude that actively steers our boat and our life. Without a positive, faith-focussed attitude, we will end up in an unintended place, or worse, we may lack the resiliency needed to bounce back from pain and hardship. Remember, using the PIES formula (Chapter Two) to define our attitude starts with being positive and will ensure we maintain a positive bearing.

Take Care of Yourself

Changes in attitude are a challenge, but support resilience and thriving. To be resilient and to thrive we must do the best we can to take care of ourselves, particularly when it comes to dealing with stress.

More and more research reveals the strong correlation between our attitude and the functions and activities of our bodies. The mind-body connection is gaining recognition in Western cultures, challenging the view that these two areas are split and separate. Eastern culture has long held that the mind and body, along with the spirit, are one entity, from which none of the three can be separated or examined alone.

Without getting into a debate of which philosophy is more accurate, we are going to look at how our attitude can affect and is affected by our body.

Note that you *do not* have to reach your destination in each of these areas before creating your RTTR attitude, but you must be moving in the right direction – striving to be as healthy as possible in each area – for your RTTR attitude to develop.

Physical Aspects of Thriving and Changing Your Attitude

I am not providing instruction on healthy activities and eating. I would be misleading everyone if I professed to have credibility in those areas. But to be resilient and thrive, we must be ready for the roars, in all ways, including physically. Engaging in physical activity has a direct impact on how resilient we are while responding to stress and managing our RTTR attitude.

We do not need to be Olympic athletes or even do any significantly strenuous exercise, but physical activity is integral to both resiliency and thriving. A healthy mind-body-spirit connection is important for success, whatever success may mean to each of us. The critical thing here is not what or how much or how long we are physically active; the critical thing is that we do the physical exercise (a Behavior in The Bearing Solution) whether we feel like it or not and that we continue to do it. Thus, we must set our attitude to exercise and let that new attitude determine our participation rather than our emotions or feelings (emotions often tend to lead us away from exercise rather than toward it, don't they?). We must follow The Bearing Solution to be ready to be resilient and thrive.

Finding Motivation

We will not be able to have a good attitude, think clearly, or participate in healthy relationships if our basic physical foundation is not solid. Our body is an amazing vessel that can regenerate, grow stronger, fight illnesses, heal itself, endure stress, and carry us along our river but it will only be able to do everything we need it to do if we take care of it regularly not just when we face a roar.

The key to caring for our fantastic physical form, that some call a temple, is our motivation. We all know that caring for our body is important, but a transfer of information does not immediately result in transformation, although it will support transforming. We know smoking is not good for us, but some of us smoke. We know that fries are not a good staple in our diet, but some still have them way too often. We know that exercise is good for us, but some of us fail to get off the couch or up from our desk to make time for exercise. Why isn't knowing the importance of our physical health enough for us to dedicate time every day to care for it the way we should?

We all have things we know we should do, or should not do, but we must find motivation that works for us. It must be something that matters more than a desire or hope. We need a purpose or goal we can be faithful to. It becomes a fire in our belly that keeps us going.

All athletic games have a goal. In North American football, there is an endzone toward which the players move the ball. They keep working even when they are losing ground. Without the endzone, without the goal, there is nothing to be faithful to. Without a reason or rationale for exercising, we will be back to our unhealthy ways and habits very quickly rather than staying committed.

Our motivation may include someone, or more than one person, who will encourage us to follow our commitment, or we can make a commitment to ourselves to take care of our physical body because we desire it; we desire to be healthy and happy or maybe our motivation is to live long enough to be involved with and spoil our grandchildren.

If you choose to have a supporter or supporters, choose those who will be in the boat paddling with you, not yelling from the shore to go faster or go harder. They don't have to do the exercise with you but should encourage you to continue and support your efforts to change and grow forward. That may not be someone close to you – sometimes the people we are closest to keep reminding us of what we were, and are resistant to anything that might change us, and therefore it requires them to change how they relate to us. The key is to find someone who understands and supports your goals and wants to help you achieve them. If you can't find someone like that, then go it alone, or call me, but keep that fire in your bones stoked and you will see your health improve.

Stress

For most people, the word *stress* immediately implies a negative feeling. However, stress itself is neither good nor bad, positive nor negative, because its interpretation depends on each person experiencing it and their situation. There are four types of stress:

1. Positive stress (eustress),

2. Negative stress (distress),

3. Cumulative stress (accumulative or chronic stress),

4. Traumatic stress (critical incident stress).

For our discussions in this section, we will be focusing on the three negative types of stress: distress, chronic stress, and critical incident stress.

Tragedy happens when we try to avoid feeling stress and pretend it doesn't exist. When we pretend stress doesn't exist, we will succumb to the river's torment without fail.

During periods of negative stress, the same chemical reactions occur no matter what the roar is: a wild animal coming towards you, a supervisor with an issue to discuss, or witnessing a critical event that shocks, disgusts, or frightens us. Everyone's definition of a crisis is different, and one person's distress should not be downgraded because another isn't impacted by the same or a similar event.

Interestingly, our chemical reactions are the same whether an event is fact or fiction. When we interpret something as negative, the chemical reactions trigger our organs to perform specific tasks for the fight, flight, freeze, and appease reaction regardless of whether the information we are receiving is true or false.

Essentially, the brain, the nervous system, and the endocrine system all play critical roles in our stress response

> The limbic system is the inner portion of the brain --
> located beneath the cortex -- and is involved in emotion, memory, and other functions. It includes the

amygdala, hippocampus, and several other structures and regions.

> The amygdala, an almond-shaped part of the brain, is activated during times of stress and triggers the raw emotion of excitement and is responsible for the fight, flight, freeze, and appease reactions.

> The hippocampus plays a vital role in learning because it is where repetition establishes responding instead of reacting during roars. It is where we form new memories, as well. It is also vulnerable to the effects of chronic stress.

> The prefrontal cortex, often referred to as the brain's executive center, is the part of the brain that enables planning and rational decision-making. It discriminates between potential rewards and punishments. It enables us to RTTR, even though our emotions and physical chemistry scream not to.

Research is showing that whether it is altruism, optimism, or moral behavior, positive attitudes trigger the same parts of the brain as the stress response, but the executive center is programmed for a reward rather than punishment and the stress is perceived as positive rather than negative, which is good for us.

This Stress Response is the same for any fear trigger. Like the teacher surprising us with a quiz, blue and red lights appearing in the rear-view mirror when we are making good time on the road, or being asked a question we don't want to answer.

If we do not get a handle on how to deal with the roars in our life, stress will start to affect our physical and mental health.

The Stress Response is an alarm system for danger and not a way to live. When the trigger is gone, or the event passes, our heart rate, blood pressure, and other bodily functions should return to normal. Indeed, going through periodic negative stress and fear

The Stress Response

Whether it is a real threat or a perceived one, negative stress invokes the same physiological response from every human body. The fear mechanism flips the switch for a fight-flight-freeze-appease reaction and the following happens within milliseconds.

1. The amygdala initiates a sense of fear or terror and starts everything rolling.
2. Adrenalin is released, which increases our heart rate while constricting our blood vessels; we feel excitement and our field of focus is narrowed.
3. The body releases cortisol.
4. Cortisol increases breathing, heart rate, and blood pressure, energy (glucose) is released into the blood stream, the muscles tense.
5. The immune system is temporarily suppressed.
6. Noradrenaline is released, counter-acting the constriction of blood vessels by adrenalin, which allows us to think more clearly and remember significant events, whether emotional or dangerous, to assist with our decision making.
7. We fight, flee, freeze, or appease based on our memories.

is important to being truly alive, experiencing life, and growing; it's when we are in chronic stress and fear that our physical and/or mental health suffer.

When the alarm system stays on because we are under constant (chronic) stress, our cortisol levels stay high and that can ruin our body's most important functions. Glucose levels in the body remain elevated, which can lead to diabetes, hypoglycemia, weight gain, or high cholesterol levels. If cortisol is consistently suppressing the immune system, people will become sick more often or more severely; thus, chronically stressed people are often sick. Chronic stress often leads to anxiety and depression, headaches, heart disease, memory and concentration problems, problems with digestion, trouble sleeping, weight gain, and many other serious illnesses.

Which forces me to ask you directly; When it comes to resilience or thriving, what about you? At even a basic level of healthcare, are you looking after yourself and not just talking about it? Do you have the medical check-ins to confirm this? I have yet to see an unhealthy leader have people who want to follow him/her.

If we work in an unhealthy workplace culture, maintain unhealthy relationships, remain unclear on what is important, eat poorly, fail to exercise, or fail to generally look after ourself, we are bound to have health issues that make dealing with the roars more difficult. The body will reach a point where it just says, "Enough. I can't do this."

That is why defining your refinable norm, focussing on thriving rather than merely surviving or staying resilient can become an issue of life and death!

Even though we share biology, our individual attitudes toward different fears do affect our biological responses differently. For some, a fear is inhibiting or even paralyzing and triggers a sense of doom, while others find it motivating and invigorating and it can be a catalyst for growth. Our attitude plays an important role in determining our response.

We can either leverage stress as an asset or allow it to weaken us. To thrive, our attitude must encourage us to face the roar, resolve our fears, and run toward them.

In his book *Over the Top*[42], Zig Ziglar shares a story that Dr. Ken McFarland delighted in telling:

> It seems a gentleman worked on the 4:00 PM to midnight shift, and he always walked home after work. One night the moon was shining so bright he decided to take a shortcut through the cemetery, which would save him roughly a half a mile walk. There were no incidents involved, so he repeated the process regularly, always following the same path. One night as he was walking

his route through the cemetery, he did not realize that during the day a grave had been dug in the very center of his path. He stepped right into the grave and immediately started desperately trying to get out. His best efforts failed him, and after a few minutes, he decided to relax and wait until morning when someone would help him out.

He sat down in the corner and was half asleep when a drunk stumbled into the grave. His arrival roused the shift worker since the drunk was desperately trying to climb out, clawing frantically at the sides. Our hero reached out his hand, touched the drunk on the leg, and said, "Friend, you can't get out of here." – But the drunkard did! Now that's motivation!

At times, we behave like the shift-worker – drifting along, not paying attention, only to fall into a hole – the result is that we feel stuck and just sit and try to tell others that they are stuck too!

Fear is a normal, human reaction causing a chemical reaction. It must never be interpreted as a sign of weakness; it is simply a reaction to an event.

To help you deal with roars and to become healthy, I suggest a Sweat, Flush, Fill, and Rest approach that will assist with stress as well as get you in good physical health.

Sweat, Flush, Fill, And Rest

Although fear is a normal reaction to an abnormal event, we cannot let stress continue unaddressed for too long without becoming ill in some way.

Prolonged stress can damage the cortex and the hippocampus. When these areas get damaged, the stress hormones don't stop flowing and this can often leave us feeling anxious and fearful most of the time.

We all deal with varying amounts of stress every day. Four steps help deal with the hormones and enzymes that are dumped into our system every day as our body reacts to stressful events: Sweat, Flush, Fill, and Rest.

Sweat

Do some physical activity. This is one of the few ways to get rid of the stress chemicals that are in the bloodstream. Walking, jogging, swimming, even housework will work. All that matters is you're doing something that causes you to sweat and is not mentally taxing. Special note here, walking a senior dog does not qualify as sweat!

As already mentioned, this is challenging because it means doing something when we do not *feel* like doing it. When the emotions are screaming at us to binge, whether it is TV, food, coffee, or other substances, we must remember our attitude and behave accordingly – we must do some exercise.

Exercise is vital because the hormones released during exercise reduce the stress hormones and chemicals. Many dread doing physical activity during stressful times but afterward, they reflect and often say, "I feel so much better after doing that."

Regular exercise brings many physical benefits. Besides the obvious ones of better heart and lung conditioning, it will increase your energy and help you focus. It builds strength and stamina to face challenges.

This does not mean we should become obsessed with exercise and expect all our stress to disappear. Healthy muscle development builds during recovery time or periods of rest. It's important to take note when your muscles reach the point of exhaustion; there is no need to exceed that point. Injury can also occur from pushing ourselves too much.

Flush

Drink healthy fluids such as water or juices to flush stress chemicals out of the bloodstream and ensure proper hydration. Traumatic stress dehydrates the brain, so water is the best fluid to consume. Caffeine and alcohol, both diuretics, will make the stress chemicals stronger. Alcohol is also a depressant, which is not good for either a stressful situation or our attitude.

There seem to be different opinions on the proper amount of water to consume each day but, in general, we need about a half-gallon (two liters) of water a day from beverages and food. The body is around 65% water. Maintaining good hydration improves our alertness, concentration, and feelings of well-being.

Fill

Fill your body with healthy nutrients. Think of food as fuel rather than a reward. Stop or reduce caffeine, sugar, and alcohol intake. Healthy food is not always what we desire but healthy fuel gives the body stronger coping abilities to deal with stressful episodes.

Also, be aware of fill when it comes to your mental intake: information, assumptions, rumors, entertainment, social media, and media reports. Don't load other stresses on top of the stress you already experience in your day.

Rest

Finally, remember to get enough rest each day. Ideally, we need six to eight hours of sleep every day, but quality is as important as quantity when it comes to sleep. Keep a routine, use relaxation techniques, banish electrical gadgets from the bedroom, don't smoke, avoid alcohol and/or caffeine, and eat lightly before bed.

Simply put REST encompasses Recreation, Envision, Sleep, and Thanks.

- Recreation – those activities, hobbies, interests that re-create us as they rejuvenate

- Envision – visualizing and setting goals for tomorrow is to have a plan for tomorrow which enables us to unload some of today's stress

- Sleep

- Thanks - gratitude for what you've done, just sitting back and noticing things to be thankful for. Often many of us (I know I do) focus on what did not get done = no REST

Emotions and Feelings

People tend to use the terms emotions and feelings interchangeably. But, in psychology and for our purposes, emotions and feelings are not the same thing. While experts agree that the two are different, the definitions they give to each vary greatly. For our purposes, we will use the definitions based on those outlined by The Emotional Intelligence Network.[43]

	Emotions	Feelings
What it is	• An immediate biological response to stimuli (anything we sense). • Chemicals are released into our body that last mere seconds. • Emotions occur without thought.	• The physical and mental sensations that arise as we internalize emotions. • Feelings are cognitively saturated emotion chemicals. • Feelings involve thought processes.
Why we experience it	• Emotions continuously regulate every living cell to adapt to emerging threats and opportunities. • They provide raw data about the world around us that is essential to our functioning, safety, survival, and growth.	• Feelings are how we begin to make meaning of emotion. • Feelings cause us to pay attention and react to perceived threats or opportunities. • We're acting on emotional data, and memories from previous experiences.

How they interact	• Emotions must precede feelings but may also occur and then fade away. • Emotions do not change; they are a physiological reaction. • Emotional reactions can be offset by training to respond rather than react.	• We must experience an emotion to develop a feeling about something or someone. • Feelings develop through various means: observations, actions, non-verbal and verbal communication, our perceptions. • Feelings can change or be changed. • Feelings take time to develop and are not only physiological. • Feelings can grow without factual verification, based on our perceptions, generating enhanced feelings which may or may not be accurate.

An older dog and a puppy were talking about happiness one day. The older dog noticed the puppy chasing his tail, so he asked what he was doing. The puppy responded, "I've discovered that my happiness is in my tail and when I catch it, I will be happy!"

The elder dog smiled and responded, "I, too, have noticed that happiness is in my tail, but I have learned that when I go about my business, happiness seems to follow me."

This story demonstrates two different attitudes about happiness. One that sees happiness as a goal and end state and another that sees it as an approach to life that ensures no matter your goals and whether you achieve them, you will always be happy. In the first case, the feeling is setting our behavior and attitude; in the second case, the attitude is setting our behavior and his feelings are following.

When we are doing activities we enjoy – playing games, working on hobbies, etc. – time seems to fly. No matter how much effort it takes to do something we love, we don't mind expending the effort. But when it's something we dislike doing, no matter how simple the task or how little time it takes, the effort seems extraordinary, and the time seems to drag on too long.

When we feel positive about an activity, our attitude starts out positive and our feelings about (and, thus, our attitude toward) the activity improve. If we feel negative about an activity, our attitude starts out negative, and our feelings about (and attitude toward) the activity grow worse, which can go on to affect our feelings and attitudes toward other things, even those we love. However, if we are focused on something we feel negative about, but we start with a positive attitude, our attitude starts positive and our feelings about (and attitude toward) the activity become more positive. We may even grow to the point of enjoying or loving the activity because our attitude has changed.

If Attitude Is So Important, Why Show Feelings?

One of the most challenging concepts of resiliency and thriving to grasp is the need to exhibit or express our feelings. This is because exposing our feelings makes us psychologically vulnerable, something scary for us and unexpected by others.

The English language fails terribly when it comes to naming and describing feelings. There's often no word(s) to name or describe many of the feelings we experience.

This is often very apparent when people try to share a sentiment or say something comforting or inspiring to those facing roars. The sympathizers mean well and want to help but the clichés and unhelpful one-liners that they utter, at often inappropriate moments, usually give little comfort.

Solomon describes this well: "Singing cheerful songs to a person with a heavy heart is like taking someone's coat in cold weather or pouring vinegar in a wound."[44]

Despite the failings of language, we must not be afraid to exhibit and talk about our feelings! To have meaningful communication, we must find people who will listen, not merely hear.

I learned this years ago with one of our sons. He was talking about his feelings, and I was only hearing him. He came close and put a hand on both of my cheeks and turned my face toward him. He then said, "Dad, listen to me with your eyes, too."

We need people who can practice listening when we have things bottled up inside. Those who will let us spit it out, sit in silence, without correcting, evaluating, or judging us. They allow us to share things that may not even make sense, so we can get beyond mere reactions by a normal human, to uncork the inner stuff so we get the real root concerns.

This is part of a problem with many crisis interventions: People do not share their emotions, feelings, and thoughts because some poorly trained clinician is trying to analyze how the client is feeling without asking them and listening. Instead of allowing the client to vent, which is cathartic and healing, the client bottles things up which we know can cause other physical and health concerns.

We need to find someone who will not try to fix things for us but will listen to connect and understand our emotions and feelings. We know there is no magic solution to fix grief and loss. Sharing with a person who does not listen with their eyes and ears can be as bad as bottling it up inside.

There is a balance, though, between the one extreme of being so overcome with feelings that we cannot think rationally and the other extreme of not having any feelings about something or someone at all.

When our feelings match the situation, we pay attention to others because we care. If we are overcome with feelings, we cannot focus and cannot help anyone. At the other end of the spectrum, if we have no feelings about something or someone, we might follow a script because we've been trained to but, because we do these things without feeling, it is obvious we don't really care. Too much or too little feeling means that thriving is not an option, survival is all that can be achieved without acknowledging our feelings.

I have started to use the term passion to refer to feelings. When we show our feelings, we are showing a passion for something. People without any passion are the saddest people in the world because they fail to acknowledge their feelings (both positive and negative). It's true, their feelings are never hurt or injured, but they also never know the feelings of joy, love, excitement, pleasure, or being truly alive.

This passage from C.S. Lewis expresses it best; I have replaced the word *love* wherever it appears with *have passion*:

> *To have passion at all is to be vulnerable. Have passion for anything and your heart will be wrung and possibly broken. If you want to make sure of keeping it intact you must give it to no one, not even an animal. Wrap it carefully round with hobbies and little luxuries; avoid all entanglements. Lock it up safe in the casket or coffin of your selfishness. But in that casket, safe, dark, motionless, airless, it will change. It will not be broken; it will become unbreakable, impenetrable, irredeemable. To have passion is to be vulnerable.*[45]

Expressing our feelings is indeed difficult if we make the mistake of letting our emotions lead our attitude. The key here is to start with attitude, behave according to that attitude and the feelings will come – they may be different than what we have felt in the past because our attitude has changed. It is important to acknowledge those feelings to ourself and express them to others as honestly as we can if communication is required.

One feeling that we have the most trouble communicating about is grief.

Grief

The term *grief* causes many of us to think about a death. But grieving occurs when we suffer a loss of any kind, not only a death: a child or parent leaving home, our home being sold or lost somehow, divorce, a pet dying or getting lost, the loss of a friendship, job loss, etc. Grief occurs when anything about which we have feelings is changed or removed. Because very few of us are taught how to grieve, when we experience losses, we don't know how to acknowledge and express our grief.

Listen and observe the number of times people express unhelpful clichés to others during times of loss. Attend to what gets said to kids, especially. One thing I often hear that worries me deeply is, "Kids are naturally resilient; they will bounce back."

Why are we encouraging kids to ignore their feelings and grieve alone? We need to teach them how to grieve so they remain healthy.

Some fear the feelings of loss so much they refuse to acknowledge the loss and their feelings about it. They become stuck in the past. Ironically, their effort to avoid grief throws them into a grief state in which they fail to move past the loss and become obsessed with rethinking and reliving the past, increasing fear, anger, and powerlessness – The Eddy Effect takes over.

Some live so focussed on the future, filled with their expectations, that they cannot live in the present. It can be expectations of a partner, spouse, boss, a child, etc. however they get caught as they neither tell the other party, nor can others always live up to other people's expectations. The result is the same series of emotions of people trying to relive the past, (fear, powerlessness, anger, etc.). Some jump ahead and regret the future they will not have – they made plans based on the loss not happening and they remain focused on what is not going to happen because of the loss – this state also stops them from grieving fully and builds fear, anger, and feelings of powerlessness – again, The Eddy Effect takes over.

Both these coping strategies are not based in realism because they both ignore the present, which is the only time during which change can occur. Dealing with loss and grief is more demanding on our RTTR ethos than anything else. The challenge is finding a way to live between the two ends of a spectrum: live in the past or live in the future and move nowhere, or live in the present, face our fears, and RTTR.

Fear

The key to addressing fear when the river journey we are on is not going as well as we want is to avoid staying in panic, or reaction, mode. Rather, we should remain faithful to our RTTR ethos. Neither panic nor drifting is an option that will lead to resilience or thriving.

Responding to storms with fear has serious fallout. Fear stifles our capacity to think and act wisely. Our Stress Response alarm system will shut down the executive center of our brain (the prefrontal cortex) if we stay in the fear emotion. As well, fear causes indecisiveness, which can mislead us.

When we look toward the future, it is important that we stay in the present, engage our attitude, and RTTR – we must face fear – to set The Bearing Solution in motion.

When the executive center is offline, or so slow that it is not firing at the same speed as the other parts of the brain, considerations like *"Is this a good idea? What is the consequence of this action? What's the plan here?"* do not get asked. If they are asked while the executive center is offline, a decision made is usually not a wise one.

When faced with the emotion and feeling of fear, we need a goal in which we have faith to strive toward – something beyond a hope or a wish. Our commitment to the goal, and any support we can get from others, will strengthen our resolve to face the fear we must to thrive through this difficult river section.

Oddly, examining non-fear-based teenagers, can demonstrate what focussing on fear can cause because in both situations, the prefrontal cortex is underperforming.

- When a human enters puberty, the prefrontal cortex is not fully engaged.

- Poor engagement affects reasoning, emotion, and self-regulation (or self-control).

- As a result, teenagers can make rash or unpredictable decisions and they can be quite moody as they are steered by emotions and feelings not attitude.

Watch what happens when an adult chews out a teenager after doing something "braindead." The adult's fear can be compounded by their lack of understanding that the prefrontal cortex is not fully operating in the teen.

Adults often get angry and raise their voices, as if the teenager is deaf. It compares to the way some people raise their voice when speaking to those who don't speak the same language: Their failure to understand it is not a hearing issue but a comprehension one.

The adult says something like, "Did you think about what might happen before you did that?"

The teenager's head will have the same tilt a dog has when they hear a strange sound. The teen looks baffled, as if they don't speak the same language. That look is often followed with something like, "Nah, why?" The ramifications of their actions have literally not crossed their mind!

What about us big kids, who – if stuck in fear or stress – have a prefrontal cortex that is also not fully operational? The same answers may come out. After all, they are a normal person with normal reactions to an abnormal event.

For example, a normal reaction to starting to spin after hitting snow or hydroplaning while driving is one of locking the arms (freezing), struggling to control the car (fighting), or letting go of the steering wheel (fleeing). Only those who have been trained to drive in snow, face the fear emotion of spinning with the correct response to keep the car on the road (or avoid the spin completely). Rather than reacting to their fear, trained drivers stay faithful to their goal of staying on the road and avoid accidents.

Another example is Lifeguard training, which requires guards to learn how to break the hold of a drowning person. People who are in fear emotion, without their executive center operating, are drowning and will grab any rescuer and can drown her/him if the guard does not stay in response mode and stay focussed on her/his goal of saving the drowning person.

One thing I have done in many contexts is develop an awareness of this fear factor when it comes to communication, feedback, or setting up a discussion about a project. Oftentimes leaders would ask a person into their office to talk about this. However, the way they asked, for example, *'John there is an issue I need to talk with you about on this project'* would actually trigger the fear reaction. The result? The leader was no longer having a discussion but felt like they were lecturing or talking to a rock. We walked through other ways to communicate, and the result was that persons would arrive ready to partner and complete the project.

Remember me mentioning that at the beginning of the COVID-19 pandemic buying toilet paper was the rage and that I almost got dragged into it as well? This is an example of our fear shutting down our prefrontal cortex: People were buying so much toilet paper yet when they were asked why they could not find any answer. Our executive centers were not working. After the panic reaction subsided, there were signs at stores stating, *"Returns on toilet paper and paper towels will not be accepted."*

Often, when a person gets a health scare, they diet, exercise, and attempt to de-stress, and things start to move in a positive direction, for two to three months, but the short-term energy that stress delivers will start to fade because the commitment, faithfulness is not there. The result of not following is the person can end up eating, drinking, or smoking more, or being less active than before the scare because they are not committed to their new regime. The human body is just not designed to maintain fear-based stress-energy, we require motivation, or faithfulness, to a greater purpose.

Without resolving our fears, our sense of self-confidence will erode to the point that we are tormented by our own feelings. The hurts and disappointments may precipitate panic. Tragically, we could become imprisoned by feelings of defeat. Think about the repercussions to a workplace in which workers are always in crisis or panic (fear) mode; the energy, creativity, and growth of that workplace cannot happen because the executive center begins to shut down. We see this during the COVID pandemic amongst healthcare personnel, particularly nurses and doctors.

There is no way around these two options during fear. We chose to live either by fear or by faithfulness. The first will lead to burnout or failure (The Eddy Effect); only the second will keep you on course (The Bearing Solution). The only way to deal with apprehension, anxiety, fear, and other feelings of threat is to face and run toward them while remaining faithful to your RTTR ethos. To be resilient and to thrive, be directed by your attitude, focus on your destiny (keep your head up and look forward), and engage your VERI partners. As Winston Churchill is quoted as saying, "When going through hell, keep going."[46]

Preparation For Roars

In between the roars, we can prepare. Prepare to face the roars we may encounter. Do this when we are in calm waters, so we are ready for the unexpected. Here are some pre-event items to work on.

Self-care is not selfish.

Self-Care

Valuing yourself does not mean that you do not value others. To care for others, you must care for yourself first. In other words, self-care *is not selfish*.

Sweat, flush, fill, and rest before the roars so you will continue to do so during the roars. If self-care is our regular practice before roars, it will remain a practice during roars.

Avoid Turtling

Turtling is a term used to describe avoidance. Although many consider it a form of self-care, it is not. A turtled boat has overturned completely; if it has a mast, the mast is pointing straight down to the river, lake, or seafloor. In many cases, people caught under the boat can find a pocket of air in which they can breathe and feel safe. The problem is they cannot see where they are going and, eventually, they will run out of air!

The turtling approach to roars is the one with which I was most comfortable. I would hide in my shell, feeling safe for as long as possible, instead of being proactive and changing the relationships, activities, lifestyle, or other habits that could be changed between and during roars.

Mental Preparation

Visualization, or imagining how to respond during a roar, based on our new RTTR ethos and RTTR attitude, is extremely useful to support our Bearing Solution, resilience, and thriving.

Mentally rehearsing our RTTR actions, following our attitude rather than our emotions, takes practice. The key question is: What is the plan when a roar catches you?

We practice this mentally because we must examine our thinking, our attitude, our ethos, and refine it so that rather than reacting as we always have, we respond. It is inner work that requires honesty with ourself, Repeating positive actions builds the thrive muscles. It may include addressing our beliefs.

Like a fire drill, lifeguard training, or first responder training, we must repeat our mental practice so that when a roar hits, we automatically respond rather than react.

Build An Action Plan

Which roars are our triggers? Identify triggers, then determine positive ways to address them. This is where our VERI partners are so essential for success because they often see options that we do not.

The factor to address is not the trigger but the response. We want to notice what person, place, situation, or thing results in a reaction – be it psychological or behavioral – and determine a positive way to respond. We cannot change our triggers, but we can change our attitude toward them and our response, which – in turn – may reduce the effect the trigger has on us.

The first stanza of the Serenity Prayer is perfect for reminding us where to focus our effort and energy: God, grant me the serenity to accept the things I cannot change, Courage to change the things I can, and Wisdom to know the difference.

Remember:
Serenity
Courage
Wisdom

Serenity (peaceful and calmness), Courage (bravery and daringness), and Wisdom (understanding and appropriateness) are vital for thriving.

Regulate Your Emotions And Feelings

Identify what is under your control and accept what is not. Learn from setbacks and failures rather than seeing only the negative.

For both things under your control and those that are not, adopt a positive attitude. Be mindful of your behaviors as well as those of others. Do not always assume that you know what other people are thinking or feeling (this is an area you cannot control, but you can ask them how they are feeling or what they are thinking so you know).

I'm not talking about more training, but these principles are vital. We must try to develop our emotional intelligence or emotion quotient (EQ). A relatively new term, EQ encompasses our ability to understand, use, and manage our feelings and also understand, motivate, and work cooperatively with others in positive ways. It involves being intentional or mindful of our behaviors and managing relationships carefully. The outcomes can be benefits like stress relief, effective communication, improved empathy for other people, and thriving through roars to name a few.

When something is important enough, you do it even if the odds are not in your favor.
Elon Musk

Delayed Gratification

Don't expect to get immediate satisfaction. When we achieve something that takes effort (and, usually, time), even if no one else thinks it's valuable, it has great value to us – we *worked for* it!

Set milestones and goals that include social outcomes, family welfare, and personal well-being. Envision how to improve your community or organization, not to mention those valuable relationships.

Realistic Self-Esteem

Be honest with yourself about your strengths and weaknesses. Having good self-esteem is not a pride problem but being unrealistic about what we can do with our talents and training is dangerous. I love to sing, so I could decide I want to be a singer; the problem is even with the right attitude, if others don't enjoy hearing me sing, I will never become a professional singer.

It is our attitude that determines what we become but we must be honest about our abilities, our strengths, and our weaknesses, to choose realistic goals.

Creativity And Sense of Humor

The gift of being able to laugh at life, at ourself, and things that do not go according to plan is precious. To be able to improvise, have some flexibility and out-of-the-box thinking starts by having a healthy, thriving attitude.

Your VERI Partners

At this point, you may be feeling a bit overwhelmed by the prospect of changing or developing your attitude. But remember, you do not have to attempt this alone. Being around people who radiate the strength of possibilities is a great way to support achieving your potential.

When we are surrounded by people who only see the negative (what can go wrong, how we can fail, life is tough and then we die, etc.), they drain us of energy and vitality very quickly. If you allow these people into your boat with you, the smallest, little river hazard can become greater than Niagara Falls without an option of a portage! And this is the role on your journey that I get hired for, where I love to serve.

Our attitude is our choice, we should never let others determine it for us! An intentionally healthy attitude allows us to make a difference in the world because when we see things in a positive light, we can influence and shape other people's attitudes as well.

Our attitude affects the impact of each event in our life, whether it's intended or not. It can be the enjoyment of life and gratitude for all our blessings, or it can birth our disappointment and anger at how things have turned out. When we assume a negative attitude, the core feeling is that neither our achievements nor our blessings will ever be good enough.

A Personal Story for Encouragement

I am still working on implementing all the practices in this attitude chapter daily. My attitude is a challenge and can become a river hazard that sometimes puts me into an eddy or up on the shore of my river journey. It is incredibly easy for me to stop any physical activity and neglect my self-care. I wallow in my feelings to the point that I feel like I am lying on the bottom of my boat, baking in the sun, and getting my head back above the gunwales to I can see where I am going is just not worth it.

How do I solve this?

I have had to choose the people who are in the boat with me (or just let someone in). For me, my family are the people while humor and love are my motivators.

We have a cottage that is easiest to access by water. One day, driving down the lake, someone asked me a question about something; I was starting to respond when they started talking about something else.

What did I do? Modeling perfect maturity, wisdom, and intelligence, I pouted!

One son looked at me and asked, "What's the matter with you, Dad?"

Continuing with this maturity, I acted like I did not hear him. He repeated it louder and I refused to respond with anything more than a gentle smile and nod.

They turned to my wife, "What's the matter with him?"

To which she replied, "Oh, whenever he gets his feelings hurt, he pouts for a while. He will be fine!"

As we neared the shore where our vehicle was parked with the boat trailer, my eldest son leaned forward and said loudly, "Hey Dad, please give me the truck keys. I will go get the truck and trailer while you are busy sorting yourself out!"

To which we all busted out laughing.

We all need people in our boat, who see the eddies when we get sucked into them. Those encouragers who love us enough to point out our eddies with encouragement rather than judgment, even with laughter when the time is right!

Moving Forward

Attitude has significant influence on our overall well-being. Attitude alone, however, is not enough to thrive. It is only one leg of the stool on which thriving sits. You cannot master your attitude alone and be resilient or thrive. The other two legs of the stool are required, *Beliefs* and *Connections* and these components will be discussed in the next two chapters.

> *Your attitude determines your altitude, not your aptitude.*
>
> Zig Ziglar

CHAPTER FIVE

B is for Beliefs

Beliefs give us focus. There are parts of the river that widen, where we cannot see the distant shores very well. For example, in parts of the river that widen into a lake where waves can blow up, like the farmer plowing a field (Chapter Three), we need something on the horizon to steer toward. To thrive, to be faithful, we must be willing to find something which gives us motivation to press on.

Have you ever noticed that when you are not sure where you are going, it seems to take forever to get there? The child's question of, "Are we *there* yet?" is something we adults can ask just as frequently, although maybe not out loud. Imagine being in a boat, tossed around in a storm, a crisis, in the middle of a lake where you cannot see the shores, and someone tells us to be patient! I'm not sure what you are like, but I won't take their words very well!

When we know what we want our destination to be, and focus on it, we can access new levels of patience, especially if it is something we truly desire. In this case, delayed gratification keeps us moving forward.

Do you know the old English word for patience? It is long-suffering. That sure puts a different perspective on patience, doesn't it?

Questioning Our Beliefs

How can we discuss resilience, mental health, and thriving without discussing what we believe?

To be blunt here, if what you think and your spirituality are not relevant to what you believe, I don't know what is. Our beliefs, our faith (even if it is atheism), are a core component of who we are as a person, and they contribute to most aspects of our lives, thoughts, and emotions.

Imagine talking with a person who believes that they do not have any friends. In conversation with them, counsellors and others try to get them to understand that this is not an accurate perception or mindset: They *do* have friends and people *do* love them, even when it doesn't feel like it. We try to help them change their perspective, but how can we achieve this without talking about their beliefs?

To be resilient and thrive, we cannot side-step subjects that are considered politically incorrect, touchy, or taboo.

We must determine for ourselves what our beliefs are. They must be able to stand up to questioning, examination, and scrutiny; we need to justify them in our own mind. Otherwise, our beliefs become a flimsy fantasy that will never support resilience and thriving through roars.

Figure 5.1 Photo of tree that has grown around benches placed at its base. Courtesy of: https://expressdigest.com/bizarre-photos-capture-trees-growing-around-unusual-items/

The growth in our beliefs, which begins at birth, is analogous to growth in a tree. When a tree is a young sapling, it has so much flexibility it is almost impossible to break it by bending it. The tree is flexible and pliable but it does bend to obstacles and influences in its environment; this is our infancy. Next, the tree may get staked to support it and guide it to grow straight or it may not be staked and may grow despite rocks, other trees, and obstacles in its way. Both trees survive and continue to grow, however these formative years will determine the direction, health, well-being, and potential of the tree. This is comparable to our childhood. Trees continue to grow and branch around their blemishes, surroundings, and neighbors as each affects the tree's strength, form, and health. Trees are said to have plasticity and our brains do as well, which neuroscience is proving.

In this analogy, we may end up holding beliefs in rules, rituals, and self-perceptions without understanding the rationales behind those beliefs. Do not misinterpret me, I'm not saying these are bad things; they may be good and may be intended for good but sometimes they result in negative beliefs.

For example, without discipline and rule-following, life would be sheer chaos. Discipline and punishment are not the same thing, however. Discipline is about growth and development of character while punishment is about penalizing unwanted behavior. Discipline teaches and is based on values while punishment teaches and is based on rules. Punishment aims for perfection while discipline aims for growth. Punishment is based in control while discipline is based in love. Punishment is reactive, negative, and external while discipline is proactive and self-monitored.

Discipline requires Love. Punishment does not require Love

The Importance Of Questioning Beliefs – Our Own And Others

I believe we can only be resilient if we test our beliefs through the questioning phase. The adolescence years are the questioning years, essentially the time for testing assumptions and defining truths to believe in and be faithful to. If this questioning phase does not happen, we can end up becoming an adult chronologically, while having a very childish belief system that doesn't stand up to roars or questioning.

If we don't question our beliefs and those of others, we may adopt beliefs that are not helpful (think of the person who thinks s/he has no friends – that belief is only hurting her/him). When we do not question our own beliefs, we will be defensive when someone challenges one or several of our beliefs.

This practice of questioning beliefs can be strengthened or thwarted depending on who is being questioned and how they react or respond. This questioning phase is critical to thriving because we grow, learn, and develop the strength to think for ourselves; we determine what we will be faithful and loyal to. That strength in our faithfulness to our beliefs allows us to RTTR.

A critical step in our maturation involves being willing to question our personal beliefs, why we believe what we do, whether we are comfortable with our beliefs, and – if not – how they must change to remain faithful to them. This questioning includes examining spiritual beliefs, morals, definitions of right and wrong, the values assigned various behaviors and motives, and what is most important in life. Our personal beliefs determine whether we succumb, survive, have resilience, or thrive in response to roars. During this process, we refine our beliefs to reflect our own dogmas, convictions, and faith.

A *long time thinking something to be true does not make it so.* This illusory truth is a proven principle, however it is a hazard for our resilience and to thriving.

Sometimes, if a question isn't answered or can't be asked at this phase, our growth is stunted. If the questions can't be asked (because authority figures don't allow them to be) or if they aren't answered (because the answer doesn't make sense or it is a ritual that has been in place so long no one can explain it), a healthy adolescent phase will seek out answers elsewhere. They will seek out places where their questions can be asked and/or answered.

This search for somewhere to ask questions and find answers can be dangerous as questioners will join a group simply because they feel heard, not because their questions are actually answered.

If people refuse to answer questioners and the questioner does not get answers, their questions get swallowed and will manifest in one of two ways: first, the questioner may disconnect and live as if they have no questions; second, the questioner may become frustrated because they are not getting answers. In the first case, the questioner will live without passion or conviction because they are not invested in their beliefs. In the second case, the questioner's frustration is usually exhibited by anger, and very reactive.

The questions must be addressed for us to be faithful to our beliefs so we can grow and thrive. That doesn't mean that we have all the answers; it means that we've done enough questioning and learning to form our own beliefs and to grow on our own.

Those secure in their beliefs and faith seldom, if ever, get defensive. If a person challenges us to prove how wrong our beliefs and convictions, are we really upset or angry? No, we will either walk away rather than argue or we will listen to them and – if they have valid arguments – we may question our beliefs again (and, perhaps, clarify them) but defending our position will not be necessary because we are committed and faithful to our personal beliefs.

A willingness to discuss issues honestly and openly allows us to learn and enhances our resiliency. Those who are closed to discussing or considering different or new ideas make resiliency difficult to maintain, never mind thriving. Thriving is impossible for these people because thriving is all about growth and an unwillingness to consider new or different ideas does not allow growth. A change in one's belief is not always necessary, but a willingness to learn is required to be resilient and thrive. Investigation and inquiry can help us answer questions, but many valuable things are also learned anecdotally or through experience.

Crooked Thinking

Beliefs have powerful influence on resilience. How many times have we heard someone say (or said ourselves) that they want to try something, but are stopped by a little voice inside them?

The "voices" express our fears (our channel markers) that we try to avoid as we travel along our river. Fears learned from others, elders, or our own experiences: *Don't get too close to the edge*, instilling a fear of heights; *obey authority* (versus respecting authority), instilling a fear of questioning; *you must get good grades to succeed*, instilling a fear of making mistakes.

Fears are triggered by a variety of beliefs, and lead to overthinking what we should do. The next thing we know, we're doing lots of things but *not* doing what we need or want to do. We are stuck in the eddy we create as we turn back-and-forth between our fears, our beliefs, and where we want or need to go.

The truths behind our beliefs are central to our values whether we adopted our beliefs from someone we trust (or trusted), developed and learned them through questioning and experience, or learned them by observing others. Although the truths may be external to ourself, we internalize them through growth and refine them through questioning. If we decide to own them after our questioning, we become committed and faithful to them.

There is a great lesson from the Apostle James:

But when you ask God, be sure that you really expect Him to tell you, for a doubtful mind will be as unsettled as a wave of the sea that is driven and tossed by the wind; and every decision you then make will be uncertain, as you turn first this way and then that. If you don't ask with faith, don't expect the Lord to give you any solid answer.[47]

I know this verse is not earth-shattering news; I expect most of us have known a person who is one way today and another way tomorrow. This is challenging because their behaviors lack a sense of consistency and commitment.

How can we remain faithful and committed to a belief if we have never identified on what it is based?

Those that waver back-and-forth, constantly changing their direction to avoid fears, and going nowhere they want to be, are practicing crooked thinking. To correct crooked thinking, we must change our beliefs from fears to a driving force of positive change and growth.

Crooked Thinking Styles

Crooked thinking comes in many forms. Many styles of crooked thinking stem from assuming the worst and self-blame. Do you recognize any of the following negative self-talk?

Personalization: Blaming oneself without knowing what, if anything, is wrong.
e.g., "My partner/parent/friend looks so upset. I must have done something wrong!"

Magnification or Minimization: Blow possible outcomes out of proportion by magnifying or minimizing them.
e.g., "I can't believe that project didn't work out. I'm sure I'll be fired!" or "I can't believe that project didn't work out. I am solely responsible for the poor outcome."

All-or-Nothing (Black and White Thinking): Anything other than perfection is failure. e.g., "If I don't score 100% on this exam, I am such a failure."

Mind Reading: Assuming to know what others are thinking.
e.g., "My HR manager wants to meet with me. I know she's thinking I'm a screw-up."

Discounting the Positives: Only focussing on the negative and none of the positive outcomes of one's actions.
e.g., "Everyone loved the get together except for ____ . I must be a bad host."

Should/Ought/Must: Blaming oneself for failing to do something you believe should/ought/must be done to be successful.

e.g., "A loving parent should/ought to/must always enjoy being with their kids. I'm a bad parent because I don't!"

Blame: Blaming oneself for every negative outcome.

e.g., "Our department missed our quota. It's all *my* fault!"

Tragically, many of these crooked thinking styles escalate when we are stressed and, during a crisis, these thoughts can get out of control and even take control.

But if we examine the beliefs that make us think that way and question them, we can start to change those beliefs and straighten out our thinking and our direction. Why do we feel so responsible for everything when, if a friend feels that way, we quickly try to illustrate how wrong they are? Very rarely is one person responsible for everything and very rarely is the outcome of someone's actions all good or all bad.

When we use crooked thinking during a crisis, we are adding to the crisis rather than running toward it. The roaring in our ears becomes so loud that we either become frantic in our actions or freeze. In either case, we are not running toward the roar; we end up either succumbing or merely surviving the roar.

To be resilient and to thrive during a crisis most of us must refine a new norm before the crisis occurs so our beliefs are the force and fuel that will compel us forward toward the roar.

Changing Our Beliefs (And Actions)

I mentioned in Attitudes (Chapter Four) how crisis can shut down the cortex and we start telling ourselves to stop thinking about the crisis. I frequently tell people immediately after a crisis to stop telling themselves to stop thinking about the crisis. I do this to point out that this is not effective. I say, "Do not think about a pink pickup truck. Block a pink pickup truck out of your mind. Whatever you do, you cannot think about a pink pickup truck!" Then I ask, "What are you thinking about?"

Can you guess their answer? What are you thinking about? So, how effective is telling ourself not to think about something going to be?

A fundamental understanding here is knowing that **resilience is not something that we do; it is something we are.** Resilience is not something we are born with or without. It is not something we do once, and it is accomplished. Being resilient requires addressing what we believe. If we fail to do this, we will find ourselves reacting rather than responding and we will find ourselves stuck in The Eddy Effect.

I love the saying, "Everybody is a genius. But if you judge a fish by its ability to climb a tree, it will live its whole life believing that it is stupid."[48] What we believe impacts our behavior, our destiny, and our ability to thrive.

> # We need to *stop listening* to ourselves and *start talking* to ourselves.

Instead of telling ourselves to stop believing our crooked thinking, we must find alternatives to that thinking and that belief. Instead of trying to *not* think about something, you must determine what you *are* going to think about instead.

Whatever we call it – talking, teaching, lecturing, encouraging, exhorting, pushing, or preaching to ourselves – we must first actively think or cogitate about our beliefs rather than simply react to a situation (and, thus, letting our emotions rule our actions and fall into The Eddy Effect). By changing our beliefs, we can then behave accordingly, so that we feel in control and sure of our course (The Bearing Solution). We do not control emotions, we control our thinking, which – in turn – triggers the feelings we want to have. Our beliefs are key to the feelings we feel. We must change our thinking and our beliefs to change our feelings and actions.

> Cogitate (v)
>
> *To ponder or mediate on intently.*
>
> *Implies deep or intense thinking.*

There are many teachings about this in spiritual and literary writings:

- "Carefully guard your thoughts because they are the source of true life"[49] And, "For as he thinks within himself, so he is."[50]

- "A man is but the product of his thoughts. What he thinks, he becomes."[51]

- "The mind is everything. What you think you become."[52]

- "I think therefore I am."[53]

- "A man is what he thinks about all day long."[54]

With all the different ways of saying pretty much the same thing, we should take note of the importance of what these scholars are saying about our thinking. It is not just the event but what we think about the event, what we believe about the event, that determines what we choose to do; our beliefs determine how we act.

For example, after a serious transit crash, people are interviewed by media and asked if they are nervous about being on another train or bus. Instead of accepting normal reactions, the question insinuates that being nervous after an incident like a crash is odd or unexpected. A normal person's reaction to surviving an accident is to be nervous when back in the same situation – if someone was *not* nervous something more serious is wrong with them! The resilient and healthy question to ask is, "What are you going to do to overcome the *normal* reactions to an *abnormal* event?"

William James, who is credited with founding positive psychology said, "Be not afraid of life. Believe that life is worth living, and your belief will help create the fact."[55] Stephen Hawking is a powerful example of this belief. A disease that normally claims victims early and leaves them in a vegetative state did not, in his case, because of his belief in what he could do. He was definitely not a passive believer!

Over and over, we are reminded that what makes humans unique is our ability to contemplate and change our thinking and beliefs.[56]

To be more resilient, to thrive through crisis or change, to live more and worry less, we must think, and we must think rightly – about the right things, at the right time, on the right wavelengths – with our antenna tuned to a truth that will encourage and fuel this. Isn't it ironic that the things we worry about seldom happen?

The Benefits of Worry

I have read in numerous posts and articles the following statistics, and whether every percentage is accurate or not, I can certainly vouch for the accuracy of the trend: 85% of what people worry about never happens and, of the 15% of things that do happen, 79% of the people realized either they could handle the difficulty better than expected or the struggle taught them something worth learning.

This means that 70% of what we worry about is caused by fear-focused beliefs that frighten us into exaggeration and misperception, instead of thinking with a faith-focused mind – the resilient mind!

Stress from worrying generates serious health problems. The stress hormones that worry produces have been connected to heart disease, some cancers, premature aging, dementia, and other physical ailments. I have seen worry add fuel to marital discord, family dysfunction, depression, not to mention poor job performance or community involvement.

When we are worried or concerned about something, we ruminate on it all day. When stressed, do we ever forget about what's causing the stress? If we can fret, worry, and stress on something all day (negative thinking), why are we not doing it for passion, values, or focus (positive thinking)? I love that term ruminate as it sounds more professional than stew, fret, or worry. It also reminds me of the old percolator coffee maker, where things just keep perking through the mind all day long, which is kind of what worrying feels like!

There are no benefits from negative projections and worrying. Instead, focus your energy on your values, positive thinking, and passion.

Although this thinking can become as persistent as worry, it is focussed on a positive direction, over things we can control.

Optimism and Pessimism

All these examples target how one looks at situations. People can write off optimism as wearing rose-coloured glasses or day-dream-type thinking, but optimism is not that simple. It is the Stockdale Paradox;[57] it is confronting the truth but also having an awareness of our own resolve, of our life force. Optimism can work like an energy source that motivates and initiates an empowered response to address difficult and stressful situations - our defining moments.

A better way to define optimism is to see it as a belief about the future – a future-oriented focus, which integrates the attitude and beliefs that things will work out in the end. Optimists believe that the future will be positive and that things will work out for the best, even if it is not what they had envisioned. Yes, discipline, hard work, and perseverance are required, but they will succeed.

Pessimists, in contrast, see the future as gloomy, even dark. They believe and expect that bad things will happen to them. Their attitude and beliefs lead them to doubt that they have the skills and strength to achieve their goals. In other words, optimists and pessimists have very different attitudes and beliefs. The important thing to remember is that attitudes and beliefs can change to the positive; it constitutes growth.

Optimism Over Pessimism

Positive psychologist Martin Seligman has noticed that when bad things happen to pessimists, words like *always* and *never* seem to flow off their tongues.[58] Statements like, "This always happens to me; I never get what I want." The negative event impacts their beliefs about all areas of their life, and they can't see an end to their sorrows.

Optimists, on the other hand, tend to think that negative events are merely blips on the radar. They don't allow negative experiences to act as a virus that will corrupt their whole operating system. Words like *occasionally, sometimes,* or *recently* punctuate their speech.

Canadian–American psychologist Albert Bandura is known as the originator of the theoretical construct of *self-efficacy,* which he describes as a *belief in one's own agency/effectiveness.*[59] His research led him to determine that optimistic people have well circumscribed problems and, further, that they view their problems as temporary exceptions to the rule. He said, "[Optimistic] people guide their lives by their beliefs of personal efficacy."[60]

Bandura observed that beliefs influence the following:

- the course of action people choose to pursue in each situation.

- how much effort they put forth in given endeavors.

- how long they will persevere in the face of obstacles and failures.

- their resilience to adversity.

- whether their thought patterns are self-hindering or self-aiding.

- how much stress and depression they experience in coping with taxing environmental demands; and,

- the level of accomplishment they realize.

Refining Optimism

Optimism allows us to see the *process* of success as valuable. That is, the work to achieve success is worthwhile, regardless of its outcome. Like refining our new norm, described in Chapter Two, refining our optimism is akin to old silver refining processes.

In the past, to refine silver, a silversmith heated up silver ore to a liquid form and burnt off impurities, a process called smelting. When it cooled down, the silversmith would look at their reflection in the silver. If the reflection was not clear and pure, like a mirror, the silver would go back into the smelting pot and into the refiner's fire. This process was repeated until the silver was so pure it perfectly reflected the face of the silversmith.

Refining our attitudes and beliefs to be optimistic is a similar process. We examine our attitudes and beliefs and "burn-out" the negative ones and then look at ourself to see the result. If we are not happy with what we see, we "burn-off" more negativity by examining the logic and faithfulness of our beliefs and attitudes. We smelt our beliefs and attitudes until we are optimistic about and committed to our process and our future.

This refining process improves our beliefs about ourselves and others. It allows us to change our understanding of a situation so that we can learn, even from a person who is always critical or has crooked thinking styles, without agreeing with their negative point of view.

Setbacks become opportunities to learn something about ourselves, our values, attitudes, beliefs, lifestyle, relationships, and other factors in our lives that change after these refining moments. These defining moments happen often and can include events like our car getting hit in a parking lot, job loss, our partner telling us our relationship is over, red and blue lights in our rear-view mirror, a uniform at the door, your boss calling you into her/his office, a doctor calling and asking to meet with us immediately, and the list continues.

Locus Of Control

There is another component of beliefs that is important, as well. First published by Julian Rotter in 1954, it is the concept of the locus of control for decision making. It identifies the tendency of people to believe that control resides either *internally* within them, or *externally* with others or the situation.

Optimists tend to have an *internal* locus of control – that is, they believe that we influence events in our lives. The difficulty for many optimists is to find a healthy balance between thinking everything is *all up to me* and the concept that something outside of themselves could have dealt them a bad hand. Optimists with a high internal locus of control believe in our own ability to control and influence the world around us. Our future is in our hands alone and our choices lead to success or failure. The downside of having a high internal locus of control is that, in accepting responsibility for the future, these optimists must take blame for failures because they believe that nothing else could be affecting the outcome of their decisions.

Those with a high *external* locus of control believe that control of events and others' actions are outside off us and we have little to no control over things. Those with a high external locus of control believe that they have no control over what happens to them because what happens is determined by others or powers outside of themselves. Sometimes they believe there is nothing they can do but obey.

An external locus of control is described as,

> The degree to which persons expect that the reinforcement or outcome is a function of chance, luck, or fate, is under the control of powerful others, or is simply unpredictable.[61]

Learned helplessness occurs when a person is conditioned into acting helpless even when control over their situation, the power to change a circumstance or outcome, is within their grasp. They just believe that they cannot do anything to affect their situation or condition. People with these beliefs can become defeatists, which makes them passive and accepting. Even success is attributed to luck, a higher power, or chance, rather than to any of their efforts.

The key thing to remember is that some people think control, power, and leadership all mean the same thing, but they do not. A leader may be great at his/her role without controlling; others can be obsessed with control of situations and/or people while not being in a leadership role at all. Leadership is not about position or title; it is about character, not what someone does or has. The litmus test is the authority or influence they have over or on others. Some people may have power or control and yet no authority in our lives. While others may have no power or control and have significant authority in our lives.

Just as there is no way that our actions and beliefs have absolutely no impact on our life, there is no way to control everything in life.

Again, the Serenity Prayer outlines this so eloquently – we must learn to accept what we cannot control and change or manage those things we can.

The balancing between our belief in an internal locus of control versus an external locus of control involves finding a healthy tension between being hard on yourself and accepting that external forces have impact on our lives. Those who constantly analyze what went wrong to improve themselves next time (not those who are looking to correct what someone else did) can sometimes come across as hard-charging, driven people who take no prisoners! While those who believe control lies outside of themselves may never accept responsibility for anything. They can be a pleasant team player when things are good, but if the results are not positive, they will be the first to complain that something external attributed to the underperformance, including blaming others on the team or externals that really couldn't have affected the outcome.

The balancing can be summarized as: **Work like everything depends on you** *and* **pray like everything depends on God.**

Your locus of control is critical as you travel your river and hit roars and hazards. Do you believe how you navigate and deal with the hazards is all up to you? Or do you believe it is all up to God? Or are you somewhere in the middle?

Character

The meaning of RTTR includes maintaining faithfulness to our values when the river gets tumultuous. In those moments, we come to understand words Paul wrote to his Roman co-believers:

> *And not only that, but let us also boast in our sufferings, knowing that suffering produces endurance, and endurance produces character, and character produces hope, and hope does not disappoint us, because...*[62]

Isn't RTTR about our faithfulness to what defines our character? Change the following word *character* to resilience or thriving

> *Consistent endurance leads to the establishment of what we all want but very few have, character! Character is sustained strength to say no to the harmful things for our lives and yes to the right things. Character is an elusive concept to those who despise suffering. Endurance is what produces true character!*[63]

Characteristics develop out of qualities that no school gives, save the credibility earned through the school of life. Character is built not on success or one event, but on consistent rowing in the same direction over an extended period of time in spite of the hazards, storms, and great places to stop.

Character produces hope. One of the greatest attributes of character is the evenness it creates in a person. It does not waver from hope to hopelessness. It does not go high and low, up and down. Many people ride a wave of hope when they are inspired but get caught in the lows of hopelessness when conditions oppose their purpose. Character stays hopeful no matter what the situation or impossibility.

That is why comments like these resonate deep within the soul:

> *Character cannot be developed in ease and quiet. Only through experience of trial and suffering can the soul be strengthened, vision cleared, ambition inspired, and success achieved."*
>
> *Helen Keller*
>
> *Be more concerned with your character than your reputation, because your character is what you really are, while your reputation is merely what others think you are."*
>
> *John Wooden*

Victimized But Not a Victim

The COVID-19 pandemic was a roar the whole world had to deal with. Some countries changed or are changing how they interact with other countries. People behave in unexpected ways – some incredibly positive and/or sacrificial and others not so much.

Many feel victimized by COVID-19 and some of the decisions that others make in response to the illness and changes that local, regional, and national governments have made in their attempts to protect people have been unpredictable. As well as feeling victimized, we may feel humble or gain a whole new perspective on what we had, what we have now, and what we will have in the future. We may feel that we will be victimized moving forward. However, although people or circumstances may victimize us, we do not have to become victims, and this is important to remember.

Cognitive Reframing

Thinking strategies to aid in thriving are important to develop before the big roars hit, before it is too late to change course. Cognitive Reframing involves looking at our cognitive distortions to create a cognitive shift. Cognitive Reframing can be negative or positive. We will be focusing on positive Cognitive Reframing.

Let me give you an example of positive reframing:

A young man, Joe, was a city camp counsellor. There was nothing distinctive about him except his smile and genuineness, combined with the long hair teenagers often grow.

The activities that he did with the kids and the ways he engaged and energized them at the same time was astute. He encouraged the ones who were a little more hesitant. He told me a few of the kids were concerned about not doing something very well so they would not try. He shared that he loved to connect with the reluctant kids and find a way to get them to take a risk and change their thinking. Joe believed it was better to try than to not try at all.

One day, his group was allowed to attend the local municipal pool. This pool was used for competitive diving as well as swimming races. Joe and his kids started swimming and joking around with each other until one of the kids challenged Joe, "Oh yah, if you think you are so special, why don't you go off the high diving board and show us how brave you are?"

Joe told them they immediately had to choose, as a group, to either go join a different group in the water or sit on the deck to watch him – but they would not be allowed in the pool alone. He laughed when he told me that they all agreed to sit on the deck.

He climbed the ladder to the 10-metre diving platform. He tiptoed out to the end like Fred Flintstone does when he's bowling. Then he did a dive with a few rotations in front of the kids. Everything went well until he got near the water and had over-rotated – some call it a belly flop.

I was thinking, *If that had been me, my shame combined with pride would have caused me to swim to the bottom of the pool and hold on to the drain.*

But Joe did something completely different.

He swam under the surface to the ladder right in front of the kids. As he started to climb out of the pool, he flipped his long hair, just like any actor in a commercial would have done, and in his loud camp voice said, "Well, that didn't go according to plan!"

The kids all laughed, even some adults chuckled, but no one made fun of him. One child asked if he would do it again and an older man sitting on the deck asked Joe if he had ever thought about getting into diving competitions. The man thought Joe was very well-qualified to dive with his blend of fearlessness and foolishness. He told Joe to ask for him if he wanted to start training as he was the provincial diving coach at the pool.

Thus, there were two ways the event was viewed, one as a funny stunt that the kids loved and respected and one as a qualified dive, showing promise and potential. The result for Joe was that the kids wanted to spend more time with him, and they tried to get their friends into his camp group, as well.

When we reframe our beliefs and stop focussing on what went wrong, even admitting when things do not go according to plan, our reframed beliefs can attract others.

One of the biggest obstacles to Cognitive Reframing is blaming all bad things in life on others or oneself. If we are not prepared to be honest with ourselves and accept that we may have some – but not all – responsibility for our situation, reframing is very difficult (that is, we must eliminate Crooked Thinking). Again, the Serenity Prayer's request for "Serenity to accept the things I cannot change ... and the Wisdom to know the difference" is important. In my counselling, I have served people who are so focussed on fighting the situation that things get worse rather than better.

Ideally, we can review our thoughts during a past event to examine our thought processes and find some cognitive distortions we have that we can change to be more positive. We may need to do this with another person, someone trusted, so that the thinking does not get caught in an eddy!

When I do career counselling, one of the first things I notice is on what people want to focus. Do they stay focussed on what they've lost – their job – or are they starting to focus on what they need to do next? In other words, are they ready to RTTR?

Of course, they need some time to process their loss, but I have met people right after a job loss and months later they are still speaking with the same anger as the day they were laid off. Remember, we cannot change what has happened, no matter how angry we are or how many times we tell our story. The tragedy is that others start to withdraw and back away from people fighting something that cannot be changed and those backing away may be the very ones who are key for support and finding new work. The Eddy Effect has begun.

The thing about Cognitive Reframing is that it is not an ability one is born with or not; it is something each of us can learn to do. We do it unconsciously to make sense of the world, but we can do it consciously, too. It can be done before, after, and *during* a roar. When we RTTR we can reframe challenging, hazardous parts of the river to see what we can learn through them. It doesn't mean we have to enjoy it, but if we are committed to being faithful and RTTR we will be able to say and believe, *I made it. I don't want to go through that again, but I would not have missed it for the world because I learned....*

Beliefs have a profound effect as they can help or hinder. Beliefs transform our thinking so, as Paul says, "And we know that God causes everything to work together for the good...who are called according to his purpose...."[64] The question is: Do you believe everything works together for good? Or just the things we like?

The challenge of reframing thought and belief patterns requires us to break out of ruts and be willing to explore new thoughts and beliefs to chart a new course. We must intentionally focus on different things. Starting with our beliefs spurs the thinking; we can create a formula for thinking, even memorize the formula, but – more importantly – our beliefs motivate us to implement our new thinking.

Reticular Activating System (RAS)

The Reticular Activating System (RAS) [65] of our brain allows us to sift through all the information we receive every second or every day and focus on those pieces that are important to us. I often say, "We always find what we are looking for," and this, basically, is RAS. If we are intentional in our beliefs, our RAS will bring instances of those beliefs to our attention, and things in our life will fall into alignment with those beliefs.

This happens all the time when we start driving a new vehicle. Regardless of the vehicle model, oftentimes we did not notice vehicles of the same make on the road before we started to drive one, then – suddenly – we start seeing them everywhere.

The same happens when we focus on our values. Until we decide what we will be faithful to, we do not notice examples of our values in practice. When we choose to commit to a value or values, we start to notice those values in others and ourselves more frequently. We also notice when someone's value(s) and ours do not align well.

For example, if we value serving others and commit to that value, we will start to notice ways to serve others. We will see opportunities for us to step up and do something. Another person, who does not value serving as much or at all, will not see the same opportunities. They may fail to offer to help and even say things like, "They did not ask me to help," or "How did you notice that they needed help as they never said anything?"

Whatever we come to value and commit to will activate our RAS to make us of aware of a sensory information related to our faith. The RAS, or guardian of the mind, is this system that allows us to screen out things that do not matter and, instead, focus on what does matter. The RAS filters out unimportant stimuli and focusses on what is important to us at the moment in three ways:

1. **Positive Focusing:** Recognizing things that are important to us. For example, a new mother hears her baby's sounds above everything else. This assists with fortifying our faithfulness to our values and beliefs.

2. **Negative Filtering:** Ignoring things that are not important to us. For example, we all filter out white noise if the cause is not important to us –a computer humming, a dog barking, a plane flying overhead, etc. This assists with ignoring information not important to our activities and can assist with filtering out Eddy Effects that can pull us off-course

3. **Individual Perceiving:** Because we all determine what is important to us individually, we will each perceive the same event/thing differently. For example, five people see an accident, or look at the same scene, and they each will have different descriptions of what they saw. To thrive or be resilient, what you focus on during events determines whether the experiences strengthen and refine who you are or hinder you.

If our beliefs are not clearly defined using PIES (Chapter Two), we end up over-filtering everything, exhausting ourselves, and fail to focus on anything. Tragically, since the important things are seldom urgent, things like health and relationships are drawn into The Eddy Effect and we become reactive.

Our beliefs determine who and what we support. Our beliefs are the power that draw us forward as we are constantly search for what's next, what matters, and to strive toward that calling and destiny. This process is called growth. Healthy growth involves filtering out negativity, focussing on positivity, and clarifying our individual filters of what matters. It is amazing how well our brains notice what we support once we're faithful to our values and beliefs.

Essentials for RTTR

To ensure our beliefs have the strength and energy to thrive or rebound through a storm, to be able to RTTR despite any hazards in our way, four things are required.

1. Grace and forgiveness

2. A power source

3. Individual recognition

4. Love

Justice, Mercy, Grace, and Forgiveness

A key theme of beliefs is the powder-keg term *forgiveness*. To understand forgiveness, we must address three topics - justice, mercy, and grace.

- Justice is getting what one deserves.

- Mercy is not getting what one deserves.

- Grace overlooks what is deserved to bestow a blessing or favor.

The difference between mercy and grace is subtle but important. Both involve kindness and compassion, but mercy involves not bestowing a justice which is deserved while grace is not bestowing the deserved justice and giving something positive to the offender. Grace requires forgiveness that mercy does not.

The topic of forgiveness is a large, powerfully challenging one. There is so much research about forgiveness that I am only skimming the surface for our purposes.

In all my years of counselling, forgiveness is the most difficult thing to help people with. There is something in us that wants others to pay when they hurt us. When others do not align with our beliefs, we may stop moving forward. We want them to align to what we believe or, if they do not and voice their opposition, we want them to have a taste of their own medicine.

Perhaps part of the struggle with forgiveness is best demonstrated by young children. Many parents have had the experience of a child being disruptive, disobedient, and stubborn. Some try talking with the child, others tell them to sit in the chair in the corner of the room, while others send them to their room. Whatever the discipline, the child is told to stay put until their attitude changes.

I remember one parent's description of his little girl when she was sent to her room. With arms folded, stomping on every stair up to her room, and then jumping onto her bed with a loud thump, the girl called down to her dad and said, "Dad, I may be in my room sitting down, but I am only sitting on the outside, I'm standing up on the inside!"

How many of us can relate to the little girl? I sure can. So often when we are disciplined, either by others or because of our faithfulness, this is the outcome; we stop misbehaving but only on the outside. On the inside, we still believe we are right or justified.

Resilience and thriving involve both standing up and sitting down on the inside. This double-edged sword depends on whether we are standing up at the right time or sitting down at the right time for the right reasons.

Forgiveness requires us to sit down on the inside despite our belief we are right or that someone needs to pay for crossing or hurting us. The normal human reaction to want justice, if focussed on too long, can cause us to get stuck in an eddy. We think we need to get justice -- or show mercy -- to move on, but we need to forgive to grow beyond this roar.

This resistance to sit down, whether it be authorities or hazards, exposes our strength and our weakness. It's a dilemma that plays a role in all the ABCs. It can take our eyes off the goal to focus on stopping to fix, correct, or ensure that someone else learns our lessons. It can also energize us when a hazard says, "You can't get past me." Inside we are saying, "Oh yah? Watch me!"

Sitting down on the inside is hard. There is a powerful element of independence in us that makes us want to do the opposite. What does it mean to be willing to sit down on the inside? In our context, I propose that it means we surrender. We surrender to align our lives, inside and out, with what we have decided to be faithful to. It means the willingness to surrender the beliefs that hinder us from being fully committed to our faith.

This white flag is a paradox in our thinking. To commit to our faith means that we must be willing to surrender to our values and focus. When we choose to surrender to our faith it will cost us, but we know that anything of value has a cost; the only question is what we are willing to pay. This relates to our definition of success (Chapter Two), as the outcome when we are faithful to our values.

When things do not go well or according to plan, forgiveness is required. We must forgive to avoid being anchored to what we feel should or should not have happened.

Forgiveness is as a gift to yourself and others. It is especially sacred when it is a gift you receive. The reality is, however, that we will not be able to forgive others if we do not forgive ourselves.

It would be nice if forgiveness were a once-and-done activity, but forgiveness is a practice we must repeat. Just like resilience, or psychological flexibility, forgiveness is a muscle that must continue to be exercised to be strong. We must observe what has happened and see things through a different lens to forgive.

Defining Forgiveness

How do we even define forgiveness? It has been misinterpreted as pretending nothing happened, sweeping things under the rug, or telling ourself to forget about it and move on. Lewis Smedes, a man who has done much work around forgiveness, has a quote that connects forgiveness with resilience, thriving through reframing and building the beliefs so we learn to live with grace: **"To forgive is to set a prisoner free and discover that the prisoner was you."**[66]

The trigger is only activated in us when we perceive harm has been done to us. Does it have the same impact on the person who did the harm? No. Only we start swirling into the eddy of wanting them to get what they deserve.

A forgiven memory is not forgotten. We cannot change the past, but we can learn from it and grow to become something different. If we keep staring at it, without forgiveness, we will eventually end up in that place, basically what gets focussed on gets done. Think of the number of parents who said that they did not want to be like their parents but after 20 years discover they are just like them.

Forgiveness does not mean there are not consequences. There must be consequences otherwise the hurtful behavior or actions can grow to impact others. Forgiveness is also not about fairness. Some offenders may never apologize, acknowledge their wrongdoing, or repent, so the decision to forgive is our own, regardless of the other party. Smedes states,

> When we forgive evil, we do not excuse it, we do not tolerate it, we do not smother it. We look the evil full in the face, call it what it is, let its horror shock and stun and enrage us, and only then do we forgive it.[67]

Forgiveness can only happen through free-will. To be resilient and thrive, to RTTR, we must forgive to define our future. When we remain bitter or angry about a real or perceived wrong, or hold onto a desire for vengeance for it, we get chained or anchored to those negative feelings and our ability to RTTR is thwarted.

There is always discussion about whether forgiveness is a decision-based, cognitive, or emotional process, however the bottom line is forgiveness usually includes three common threads:

1. Gaining a more neutral perspective of what happened and the other person.

2. Reducing the negative thoughts and feelings toward the other person even to the point of increasing compassion.

3. Reducing thoughts and feelings demanding punishment and/or restitution.

In the same way that those grieving are told to be strong (as if showing emotion is weak), some people have the idea that practicing forgiveness is weak. But staying angry, resenting what has happened, is easy – in the short term. To forgive takes effort and work, more work than staying stuck in unforgiveness. The struggle of surrendering what we want in the moment, based in normal human reactions, to stay faithful and loyal to our long-term values takes strength. Drifting or coasting into an eddy of anger or bitterness is easy.

Over and over, we are shown that there are costs to our choices. Staying angry, offended, and bitter comes at a cost. As we've already discussed, these negative feelings have a detrimental impact on our physical, mental, spiritual, emotional, and relationship health.

Any discussion of forgiveness usually involves a discussion of spirituality. Did you know that religion has been considered a symptom of mental illness and religious beliefs and practices have been combined with pathologies? Yet, a healthy belief or faith can heal our stress over finances, health, and other daily concerns, as demonstrated in research on spiritual practice and its effects on blood pressure, recovery, mortality, immunity, lifestyle (lower suicide rates, less alcohol/drug abuse, lower criminal behaviors), etc.

How to differentiate an unhealthy, false religion or belief from a healthy religion or belief is simple. A false religion or belief is one that can never be attained or satisfied. The easiest examples are things like physical features, money, education, titles, possessions, etc.

When no limit is possible, people often become consumed by these false beliefs: if I only had more money, if I only were more beautiful, if I only were more muscular, if I only had more education, etc., I would be ok. For these values, there is no point where one feels they have done enough and, tragically, many people get caught in eddies as they lose sight of their destiny and maintain a temporal faithfulness.

Resilience and thriving involve defining wealth in a way that is something of value to you that does not cost money; something to which you can remain faithful (friendship, helping others, being healthy, etc.) This is a very important element of resilience, to RTTR, as we must be willing to think about our beliefs.

Thinking of our river journey and the hazards we must navigate, Paul wrote to one he was mentoring named Timothy that "...people who want to get rich keep toppling into temptation and are trapped by many stupid and harmful desires that plunge them into destruction and ruin." [68] Paul's words are both a reminder to be faithful and to remind others to be faithful, as well.

Justice, Mercy, And Grace

Justice, mercy, and grace are captivating concepts. People frequently say they demand justice, but what could ever make right the wrong that has been done. Getting justice involves treating others equitably in a legal sense. In theory, justice entails freeing or punishing a person based on the evidence of the case without considering the accused's gender, race, or social status. This approach assures that those who do wrong get punished and those in the right have protection. In practice, however, there are many exceptions to these outcomes in which those doing wrong are set free and those who thought they were doing right have been penalized. Justice is great in theory but can quickly become an eddy, dragging us down.

People spend time, resources, and energy pursuing justice, but often the expectations of what justice will look like does not match with what the system can deliver. Even when stolen things are returned, it does not change the impact of the theft. Talk with someone whose home has been broken into, and even though they get their content back, there is the spiritual and psychological impact. Their belief in the safety of their home has been walloped. We can become obsessed with pushing for the justice we think is deserved and get locked into a never-ending spiral.

Mercy and grace are often used interchangeably but – although similar – they are not the same thing. Mercy is the withholding of a penalty that is deserved. As I mentioned, mercy is not getting what one deserves.

Grace occurs when we not only receive mercy, but we also receive additional kindnesses on top of mercy. Grace involves providing undeserved favor. The Greek word is *charis*, which can also mean blessing or kindness. Grace is not just being spared but also being favored with good things or actions.

Mercy and grace are demonstrated by the bishop character in Les Misérables. At the beginning of the story, Jean Valjean is caught stealing several silver candlesticks from the bishop's home. When Valjean was being taken to prison to be hung, he was brought before the bishop. The bishop took mercy on Jean Valjean and did not press charges – he told the officers that he had given Valjean the candlesticks. The bishop then goes further and exhibits grace toward Valjean by giving him more silver to sell so that he can start his life over.

In the chasm between mercy and grace we find forgiveness. Many people show mercy to others, but few go on to practice grace. Grace requires a whole different level of empathy; it requires forgiveness. Most world religions have a theme of what is commonly called The Golden

Rule. There is only one that words it in a positive, proactive way, which requires the grace-based ethos. It's worded either positively or negatively, saying things like: *Do not treat others in ways that you would not like to be treated* or *Do unto others as you would have others do unto you.* My grandma would say, "You catch more flies with honey than vinegar."

A grace-based approach is the most challenging approach of the three. Regardless of how the recipients respond to our grace, we have to treat them as we would like to be treated if in their shoes. We must be careful to remember that we do unto them not in the belief that they will do unto us in the same way. Acting with the expectation of reciprocal treatment is not practicing grace, it is practicing a barter system. We must forgive them fully and without any promise of receiving any particular favor from them in the future. Doing so ensures we remain free and passionate to continue to grow because our beliefs are not tied to their behavior but to our focus.

The willingness to look at one's beliefs head on is challenging. I get it. While mercy is very, very special, grace is obviously the most extraordinary act.

To be resilient, to thrive, means extending grace-based forgiveness. The kind where you believe your destiny calls you to RTTR and the least you can do on the journey is to help another find their footing, get their capsized boat righted, but we must not get stuck in the eddies of other people's behaviors. I have taught many times that we promote prejudice when we do not teach what others believe. The normal human reaction to what we do not understand is fear. When we fear something, we want to protect ourselves. So, when it comes to interacting with other people we don't know, it is only natural to be biased. Tragically, without grace, fear or distrust does not change and we will continue to judge other events, people, and behaviors through our beliefs. Not only are others different from us, they are not free to be who they are, so we also get stuck in judgement.

For example, a parent who is displeased with a new policy at their child's school calls to express their concerns. When they reach the secretary, their anger and language, if displayed publicly, could lead to charges of harassment or similar. As the next person to speak to the same administrator, you find her/him to be curt, even cold, almost rude. You immediately begin to judge the secretary: You may determine, *"S/he has no excuse to treat me this way,"* and ask to speak with the Principal (getting justice). Or you let it slide, believing that s/he is having a tough day (giving mercy). Or, you may practice grace and extend an olive branch by saying, "It sounds like you're have a tough day and I do not want to add more to your plate, *so I....*" Grace is extending the treatment that you would want to receive after a strip has been torn off you.

Maybe you see a very formally dressed fellow shopping at a hardware store. In judgement, people are gawking and pointing. The fact that this is the first time he has left his home due to mental health challenges doesn't cross their minds. None of them understand how special this moment is for him. So rather than smiling and saying hello and wishing him a great day (practicing grace), he is stared at (justice) or uncomfortably tolerated (mercy).

The list goes on, but I hope you see my point. There is a recurring theme in social media posts about being kind to others as we do not know what they are going through. We all have our days or moments that we need to just get through it; imagine if others judged us solely by those days and moments.

Justice might mean that someone gets their consequences. Mercy may mean that we ignore or sweep it under the carpet. But when grace is offered and we allow people to be what they are, normal human beings, we start to allow ourselves to live with the same freedom.

Forgiveness sets us free. Running toward the roar requires practicing grace toward those we meet along our journey and, in doing so, perhaps being blessed ourself. When we fail to forgive and practice grace, we not only deny others; we create a hazard in our own path that can quickly become an eddy.

Practicing forgiveness and grace is not easy. Afterall, if grace was easy to provide, everyone would be doing it. How do we forgive when something wrong has happened? How do we apply the balm of grace, so we do not fall into an eddy? We must address all our beliefs – not just our cognitive component but our spiritual reality also.

Dan Cohen, assistant teaching professor of religious studies at the University of Missouri, explains,

> In many ways, the results of our study support the idea that spirituality functions as a personality trait. With increased spirituality people reduce their sense of self and feel a greater sense of oneness and connectedness with the rest of the universe. What was interesting was that frequency of participation in religious activities or the perceived degree of congregational support was not found to be significant in the relationships between personality, spirituality, religion and health. [69]:

The team examined the results of three surveys to determine if there is any correlation between self-reported mental and physical health, personality factors, and spirituality in Buddhists, Muslims, Jews, Catholics, and Protestants. They found that in all five faiths, spirituality was associated with better mental health, specifically lower levels of neuroticism and greater extroversion. The only spiritual trait predictive of mental health, after personality variables were considered, was forgiveness.

Cohen continued:

> Our prior research shows that the mental health of people recovering from different medical conditions, such as cancer, stroke, spinal cord injury and traumatic brain injury, appears to be related significantly to positive spiritual beliefs and especially congregational support and spiritual interventions. Spiritual beliefs may be a coping device to help individuals deal emotionally with stress.

According to Cohen, spirituality could help an individual's mental health by lowering their self-centredness and developing their sense of belonging to a larger whole.

I like what Dr. George S. Everly Jr. said in a course I attended, **"Faith is that which allows you to accept that which you cannot understand."**

Another author, in about 65 CE, a man named Paul – no last name – is quoted as having stated two things with respect to faith (i.e., spirituality): "Now faith is confidence in what we hope for and assurance about what we do not see."[70]

He also wrote,

> ... as we look not to the things that are seen but to the things that are unseen. For the things that are seen are transient, but the things that are unseen are eternal.[71]

A healthy and productive belief must be rooted in encouragement, understanding, and a willingness to follow it when we get into trouble. Beliefs must be addressed and be able to stand our questioning because, when crises hit, we need assurance we are standing on something solid.

For crisis, please ensure that whatever you believe can provide things that money cannot buy – to restore your spirit so you can breathe – love, joy, peace, patience, kindness, goodness, faithfulness, gentleness, and self-control.

It is vital that we ensure that we have healthy beliefs. I do hope that at some point you believe that we are more than the sum of our past! You can call this forgiveness, acceptance, or love. I just don't want people to think that paddling to get down the river is because of concerns about what happened onshore back there!

I believe: **Our past explains our present but doesn't excuse it, and it doesn't determine our future.**

Said Ray Pennings, Executive Vice-president of the think tank Cardus:

> We have a society that has a secular government, and there is a general assumption of faith being very private. On the other hand, when you actually take a look at everyday society, the

majority of people are people of faith to one degree or another, and faith informs and influences many of the ways we deal with each other on a day-to-day basis.[72]

Not only do we need to ensure our beliefs have the strength and energy to rebound after or thrive through a storm, we also need to address our motivation. We must develop, nurture, and/or strengthen the power source of our beliefs.

Our Power Source

We need to find something that *empowers* us to stand strong. Not to act callously or imperviously but to simply draw energy from when we are tired and weak. It empowers our resilience so we can move on to thrive. Similar to the keel of a boat, our power source keeps us upright and as stable as possible in stormy times. It keeps us steady in the worst roars and helps us stay stable or move forward when the conditions seem overwhelming.

Whether we call it trusting in God or another form of spirituality, our power source needs to be something greater than just normal human accomplishment or strength. To RTTR, we require an energy source that will charge, and keep charged, our battery. At the same time, the source must encourage, invite, and engage us to continue the journey. It must fuel two life-giving qualities to RTTR:

- It must provide the fuel for us to forgive. It must ensure we not only provide grace to another person or situation but also to ourself, so we do not get stalled or caught up in an eddy.

- It must provide a sense of direction. When you and I have a sense of purpose or calling we are far more likely to press on. Our power source provides both the motivation behind this purpose (the *why*) and a directional sense for us to set our bearing. Imagine trying to navigate toward your purpose, toward a destiny, but every time you check your compass it has changed? A power source for resilience and thriving is consistent and steady, even though as our understanding grows, change happens. For example, when you first put your boat in the river you may understand the importance of your compass bearing, or even that sense of a positive new norm. yet once you cross through some hazards, some eddies, and see what you have been able to achieve as you RTTR, the depth of your faithfulness will take on deeper awareness and meaning.

Our power source must be one that grows stronger as we take the next step in our faithfulness journey. While drawing us forward, it needs to also provide the foundation and acceptance of whatever point we are at along our river journey.

When we face roars, for hazards and crises always come, we must have a source of energy to help us face and move through the roars in a manner beyond just endurance. Endurance is staying in one place and continuing to withstand something. Resilience involves not only withstanding something but also moving past it. Our power source must do more than help us endure (a strong will can do that), it must empower us to move *past* endurance into resilience and thriving.

Our beliefs are what empower us. It is impossible to think the same way, have the same mindset, and still expect different results! That is all part of a new norm. We must change our beliefs to empower ourselves to get different results.

Coaching

There is an assumption within the practice of life-coaching: *The answer(s) lie(s) within the person.* The goal of good life-coaching is to help a person discover, not be told, their answer or answers.

Whatever we call our internal energy – e.g., our spirit, our soul – it is essentially the body's inclination to survive – hopefully thrive. Many sources are showing that we either hinder or help this natural energy depending on our attitudes, beliefs, and connections (ABCs). Crisis intervention often works because it unties knots – mental, emotional, cognitive, spiritual, or moral – that normal, clinical approaches cannot. It allows a person to see life in a childlike (not childish) way by examining their beliefs and learning that what they believe can be either limiting or life-giving.

If we want to stand on the shore, to avoid living life, to disengage from the journey to remain safe, then we do not need to think about our beliefs. For we will not ever choose to RTTR; we will not thrive. We need not worry about resilience and *being* resilient. Why would we need resilience if we are avoiding challenges? We would just run away and avoid the challenge. We avoid challenges but we will not travel very far or do very much in our life either.

There are some **upsides to being a victim and remaining stuck.** I hope, by naming the elephant in the room, I will challenge you to stay in your river and not become (or stay) a victim.

What is the elephant?

Being a victim allows a person to gain attention from those who want to help. This creates a false sense of acceptance in which the victim believes the pity and kindness they are receiving is indicative of love. The greater the suffering, the greater the kindness to them. They start to believe others are the key to getting through life, that they cannot thrive without the help of others.

If a victim does not take any risks or responsibility for their situation, their failure, change, or rejection can be blamed on others. By blaming someone or something for the events that occur, victims can deny personal ownership or responsibility for making decisions.

To move off the shore, away from the safe zone, which often resembles an eddy, we have to deal with the wrongs, events, and/or roars that make us want to stay there. In *The Power of Bad* authors Tierney and Baumeister examine the huge influence of bad prospects on our actions.

They describe a phenomenon in American NFL football: Many coaches study the smallest statistic to find every possible advantage for winning. The authors found that coaches frequently do the same negative thing repeatedly during games. In fourth-down-and-short situations, when the team only needs to gain a short distance to get another first down, nine times out of ten, they choose to try to avoid losing by sending in their punter to kick to the other team rather than taking the riskier option of attempting to gain the first-down.

The authors' research illustrates that the better strategy is to go for the short distance and have success. So why do so many coaches punt on a fourth-down? Tierney and Baumeister concluded there's another factor involved called the power of bad, during which our brains are wired to give more importance to negative events than positive ones. Thus, the risk of a bad outcome influences our decision-making more than the possibility of a positive outcome. That means no matter how much we want to succeed, avoiding bad events can easily become our primary goal.[73]

In the football example, if the team attempts the riskier play of trying to gain a first-down and not only fails but turns over the ball during the play and the other team goes on to score or win, the unforgiving press and fans will be relentless, and blame that one play for the loss. This risk of failure is so powerful that the coach plays it safe. The fear of failure has lost many a game.

To RTTR, we must address the risk of playing it safe, or getting caught in an eddy, by finding that positive influencer, our power source.

> *The greatest challenge in life is in discovering who you are.*
> *The second greatest is being happy with what you find.*
>
> Oscar Auliq-Ice

Individual Recognition

We know that the Pollyanna approach to life – blind optimism – doesn't work. But *resilient* optimists rarely ignore the negative aspects of life.

In their book *The Resilience Factor*, Karen Reivich and Andrew Shatte refer to this as "realistic optimism." [74]

Like pessimists, realistic optimists pay close attention to negative information relevant to the problems they face. However, unlike pessimists, they do not remain focused on the negative. Yes, I know, it is the *courage* (to change what you can) and *serenity* (to accept what you cannot change) and *wisdom* (to know the difference) aspects of the serenity prayer.

What makes a significant impact on optimism is our mindset (our beliefs). I think the easiest way to illustrate this is using the decades of research and ideas cultivated by world-renowned Stanford University psychologist Carol Dweck. She says:

> *In a fixed mindset, people believe their basic qualities, like their intelligence or talent, are simply fixed traits. They spend their time documenting their intelligence or talent instead of developing them. They also believe that talent alone creates success – without effort.*
>
> *In a growth mindset, people believe that their most basic abilities can be developed through dedication and hard work – brains and talent are just the starting point. This view creates a love of learning and a resilience that is essential for great accomplishment.* [75]

To thrive, we must believe we have influence on our growth. A fixed mindset does not allow any of our efforts, or lack thereof, any responsibility for our situation. We must feel responsible for what we do and achieve. We must be careful not to rationalize our situations by justifying our behavior with reasons that hide our actual motivations.

	Fixed Mindset	Growth Mindset
Intelligence is...	Immutable – given by genetics, chance, or God.	Mutable – can be developed, improved, and expanded.
Life is...	A test where we have to prove ourselves.	A journey where we get to improve ourselves.
The primary concern is...	Managing others' impressions.	Exploring one's own curiosity.
Failure...	Demonstrates a lack of ability, unworthiness.	Presents an opportunity for feedback.
Challenge...	Generates fear.	Creates excitement and eagerness for learning.
Effort...	Shouldn't be needed.	Is the key to improving ourselves.
Others' success...	Diminishes, exposes, or shames us.	Lifts us up, offers a chance to learn and grow from greatness.
The end result is...	An early plateau where one never reaches one's full potential.	Ever-higher levels of achievement and a greater sense of internal locus of control.

Figure 5.2: **Fixed Versus Growth Mindset.** This chart compares the beliefs of those who have resilience and can thrive (Growth Mindset) and those who struggle to stay resilient, and rarely thrive (Fixed Mindset). Take a moment to review the table and honestly place yourself in the Fixed or Growth column for each statement. This will be a starting point for you – it will tell you what you must address to be faithful and thrive (see the Discovery Guide for more).

Beliefs – Religious, Spiritual – and Coping

The word *religion* comes from the Latin word *religare*, which means *to bind*, as in binding one thing with another, such as social support, food, emotions, and morals.

The term *spirituality* comes from the Latin *spiritus*, meaning *breath*, and involves opening our hearts and cultivating our capacity to experience awe and reverence with deep gratitude. I heard something recently that described the feeling of discouragement as *suffocating*. How many can relate to that description when we feel discouraged?

On the other hand, when our spirit is full, we can just admire the view, watch children play, observe nature, look at paintings and pictures, or so many other things and be refreshed. There is a sense of awe, gratitude, and respect as we observe and see how many remarkable things are in our sphere of influence.

Combining a spirit of gratitude (providing air to suffocating lungs) with the power of community is what religion was originally about, some would say. Regardless of whether this is true or not, somewhere along the way, for some, this translated into a focus on behaviors and practices rather than the ethos or values behind them. This might be why so many of us practice spirituality but not religion. Ironically, in the cognitive/psychological fields, practitioners do not know whether to embrace spirituality or leave it alone. The result is that few clinicians discuss spirituality with their clients although many discuss community (commonly called a tribe today).

Psychology tends to sidestep spirituality because many, upon hearing the word, become fearful and react with avoidance or arguments (i.e., flight or fight). There is a world of difference between religious and spiritual faith. When religion is used for coping, it is frequently not helpful because what looks like a Bearing Solution can end up taking on an Eddy Effect and we end up right where we started.

Many who follow a purely religious faith may believe that gods are punitive and judgmental, instead of one of grace or love. This belief often creates a mindset that we deserve our troubles. When we feel we deserve our troubles, it is very difficult to be resilient, let alone thrive. We become focused on behaviors and being good rather than the ethos of the religion. I am pretty sure I am not the only one who isn't perfect all the time.

To thrive, we must define a personal belief system that is not based on our own thoughts and feelings, which can and do change, but based in an ethos that adds air to our lungs. The ethos-based belief system allows us to breath and continue our path and journey with faithfulness when our lungs are constricted by discouragement.

Love

Most of us will have spells where we are discouraged and may feel unloved. When other people fail us, we need to identify someone/something that provides us with consistent love: A source of love that will never un-love us. Acknowledging personal responsibility for this is foundational in becoming a mature, thriving adult.

Doing this will challenge some to think about our own beliefs around resilience. The best part of identifying this type of love involves pruning our belief system. Discovering real love requires accepting that we *are* human beings and subject to imperfection.

It is vital to start thinking about being *I am* in an *I have* world. In societies of ownership, toys, and treasures or power, prestige, and position, we must believe in who we *are* rather than what we *have*. Who a person is (their attitude, beliefs, values, and behaviors) makes a person trustworthy and powerful in their life, rather than any title, prestigious position, or affluence they hold.

When we allow ourselves to be childlike, we feel different expressions of love. In Greek, there are four versions of love: *agape, phileos, storge, eros.* When I speak of the loves here, I am speaking of the highest forms of love that not many of us have experienced. Experience does not change the definition; it can only impact the perspective of the meaning.

Agape is the most divine of the loves. Agape love is perfect, unconditional, sacrificial, and pure. It is not something offered by humans but is something to which humans can aspire. It is something worthy of achievement. It is love in which the giver voluntarily accepts hardship, discomfort, even death, for the loved without *anything* expected in return. In some ways, we can only honor, as in Remembrance and Veterans Day, those who loved sacrificially and without expectation of anything in return.

Philia is the word used in the name of the city of brotherly love – Philadelphia. It describes the powerful, emotional bond seen in deep friendships. It is the love that incorporates the love for other humans, addressing a care, respect, and compassion for people in need.

Storge is the word for family love. The deep bond that develops naturally between husbands and wives, parents and children, siblings, etc.

Eros is the Greek word for sensual or erotic love, sexual desire, physical attraction, and physical love. It comes from the mythological Greek god of love, Eros, son of Aphrodite, whose Roman counterpart was Cupid, son of Venus.

The proof of love is acceptance of who you are. When loved (or loving), it is not necessary to apologize for what is important to you or for saying *yes* to something you believe in. Saying yes to your beliefs does not mean you are saying *no* to others' beliefs. A love of the trees, hills, or fresh snow on the ground or the joy that comes into our soul when we hear a song that makes us sense something sacred in life, that place where passion and depth of a relationship does not even need words – that is real love.

I had the privilege of observing this between my in-laws before they both died. Even with dementia, they could look at one another and we felt we were witnessing a very sacred moment. Those moments, which feed the soul, the significant highs where we declare, "It does not get better than this," are real love. This is sometimes followed with someone asking for words to describe it. Strangely, special moments are often impossible to put into words and – if we do find words – the descriptions fall short of the specialness we experience.

We need to nurture relationships with promising people. Just like a yawn, optimism and pessimism can be contagious. It is so beneficial to intentionally surround yourself with people who are positive, confident, encouraging, and loving. This is the real love that we must find.

These types are actively living their lives as human beings, not busy being a human doing! They are in the river themselves, they will love to support you, but they will not get out of their boat and try to convince you to get into the river with your boat. They are living it and not talking about it!

How does one get things started to lay a solid foundation of beliefs? Whatever your individual circumstances may be, there are many ways to explore the beliefs dimension of life and how it can serve as a source of resilience.

Put Actions in Your Steps

Why do I believe what I do? It allows things that happen in my journey to be reframed into the knowledge that who I believe in has complete control. That does not mean they are the cause of challenges, but that I am never alone in the challenge.

I truly hope that this is not a transfer of information but a transformation for you. A fulfilling life cannot be had sitting on the shore or drifting along. It only happens when you start defining what needs to be rowed toward and keep refining it as you travel.

Some practices to assist you with examining your beliefs are listed here to get you started but they are not the only ways to explore your beliefs. Perhaps, start with these methods and look for others – they will come to you once you start the work.

Contemplation, Reflection, Meditation or Prayer

What stirs your soul, brings tears to your eyes, and bounce to your step? Whether it is music, time in nature, art, feeding birds, or something else, find an activity that allows you to practice contemplation, reflection, meditation, or prayer. A time during which your mind can ponder or muse about your experiences and behaviors. To have any real value, it should be structured to ensure it is integrated into our daily routine and practiced regularly.

Set aside a time for prayer or meditation as part of your daily routine. This is often first thing in the morning, last thing at night, or both. During this time, you need to focus on what you are sailing toward, to confirm that you are already, or are becoming, the person you want to be. The quote that illustrates this perfectly is from *Alice in Wonderland* when the cat says to Alice, "If you don't know where you are going, then any road will take your there."

It is wise and prudent to have a plan but, as it has been said before, life is the thing that happens while we are busy making other plans! Realize that there may be detours or even remapping of your journey, but you must take time each day to calmly reflect on what you have experienced, what you have learned, and how you have changed.

Spiritual Reading

It is vital to find something that speaks to you, but it is as equally important that it does not repeat what you are already thinking. For growth to happen, we must be willing to undertake things that challenge the status quo. My thinking is the Bible gives perspective. I also believe that the reading must challenge a person to think outside of themselves. This, when combined with things like time in nature or poetry (writing and/or reading), allows healing

At the end of the day, this needs to be your list and not an imposed one. It must be an activity that is not passive but rather challenges and feeds the spirit. Make a regular habit of reading scriptures, sacred texts, or other writings pertaining to your chosen faith or practice. Designate a physical location for your daily spiritual practice. This may be a room or smaller space in your home or a location in nature. It might even be in your car.

This could also include physical expression through yoga, liturgical dance, martial arts, or many other expressions like these. It can also be expressed in creative forms, which include singing, playing sacred music, writing poetry, drawing, or painting.

Time in Nature

Solitary confinement in a self-imposed prison or cabin-fever in the woods do not demonstrate well-being. People often say that being near water, a river, or a stream is relaxing. Perhaps this is why fountains and water flowing over rocks are so popular in our backyards and in our homes. There is value in allowing our boat to drift a bit or pull it to shore and just pause to celebrate, reflect, and recharge.

Humor

Find a way to have good humor each day. Good humor involves allowing oneself to see life through a different lens. Great humor should never be about putting another person down or being sarcastic. Attend a wedding where they open the floor for toasts, and someone starts to share a demeaning story about the bride or groom that they think is funny while the guests are aching for the person on the receiving end. Some think it is funny but not everyone is laughing. Great humor does not offend or putdown others; everyone finds it funny.

Invest in Yourself

This could mean taking up or restarting hobbies or taking on new learning. Choose things that recharge you. Remember that self-care is never selfish. Take a moment while having dinner with people you care about and share what you most value about the person(s) at the table. It can feel awkward, but it is so rewarding for everyone! Take time to remind yourself of some of your positive attributes and take responsibility for living as yourself.

Become Part of a Group or Community

Part of the reason that Royal Canadian Legions or groups like Alcoholics Anonymous (AA) work has to do with the power of groups.

Finding a group, or community, that worships or practices together, can give you something you didn't know you were missing – a sense of belonging, shared experiences, like-mindedness, etc. You can find groups such as a fellowship, meditation or prayer circle group, book or sacred scripture study group, or other expressions. This may be a physical group that meets at a designated location or an online community. We'll take a closer look at the types of connections made in these communities or groups in the next chapter.

A Final Story

In *The Pendulum*, Ken Davis shares a story that finishes the beliefs section well.[76] What do you believe while you're in your boat and a wave is about to broadside you?

> In college I was asked to prepare a lesson to teach my speech class. We were to be graded on our creativity and ability to drive home a point in a memorable way. The title of my talk was, "The Law of the Pendulum." I spent 20 minutes carefully teaching the physical principle that governs a swinging pendulum.
>
> The law of the pendulum is: A pendulum can never return to a point higher than the point from which it was released. Because of friction and gravity, when the pendulum returns, it will fall short of its original release point. Each time it swings it makes less and less of an arc, until finally it is at rest. This point of rest is called the state of equilibrium, where all forces acting on the pendulum are equal.
>
> I attached a three-foot string to a child's toy top and secured it to the top of the blackboard with a thumbtack. I pulled the top to one side and made a mark on the blackboard where I let it go. Each time it swung back I made a new mark. It took less than a minute

RUN TOWARD THE ROAR

for the top to complete its swinging and come to rest. When I finished the demonstration, the markings on the blackboard proved my thesis.

I then asked how many people in the room BELIEVED the law of the pendulum was true. All of my classmates raised their hands, so did the teacher. He started to walk to the front of the room thinking the class was over. In reality, it had just begun. Hanging from the steel ceiling beams in the middle of the room was a large, crude but functional pendulum (250 pounds of metal weights tied to four strands of 500-pound test parachute cord.).

I invited the instructor to climb up on a table and sit in a chair with the back of his head against a cement wall. Then I brought the 250 pounds of metal up to his nose. Holding the huge pendulum just a fraction of an inch from his face, I once again explained the law of the pendulum he had applauded only moments before, "If the law of the pendulum is true, then when I release this mass of metal, it will swing across the room and return short of the release point. Your nose will be in no danger."

After that final restatement of this law, I looked him in the eye and asked, "Sir, do you believe this law is true?"

There was a long pause. Huge beads of sweat formed on his upper lip and then weakly he nodded and whispered, "Yes."

I released the pendulum. It made a swishing sound as it arced across the room. At the far end of its swing, it paused momentarily and started back. I never saw a man move so fast in my life. He literally dived from the table. Deftly stepping around the still-swinging pendulum, I asked the class, "Does he believe in the law of the pendulum?"

The students unanimously answered, "NO!"

Human nature prefers a state of equilibrium where everything is still. Growth will only happen when there is a force challenging us to be in motion. That is your beliefs. The Instructor didn't believe the Law of the Pendulum enough to stay seated. His belief that the pendulum would swing just as high or higher than the point from which it was dropped was stronger than the new belief in the new law introduced a few minutes earlier. He was impelled to move because of his belief rather than his knowledge. This is the power of beliefs.

How do your beliefs strengthen your faithfulness? What thinking and spirituality will carry you through the hazards and keep you rowing when the water is calm? What beliefs will keep you running toward the roar?

CHAPTER SIX

C Is for Connections

Fairy tales do not tell children the dragons exist. Children already know that dragons exist. Fairy tales tell children the dragons can be killed.

G.K. Chesterton

When we teach children that a monster can be defeated, they can start to be convinced that anything else that frightens them can also be defeated.

Courage is the ability to handle fear and rejection. For courage to be realized, it must be lived or demonstrated in the presence of fear and rejection. To put it another way, playing it safe, striving to live without fear, means there is no courage. We must have courage to address the core of our connections for it is there -- deep in our souls – that we must face the fears, loneliness, and rejections we experience and deal with them to live a fuller, more satisfying life.

As adults, we think we have outgrown dragons and monsters under the bed. However, we soon start trying to keep up with the Jones and the dragons and monsters reappear! They simply manifest in different forms.

How do we handle the new monsters? What about the monster that keeps us captive in their den while others carry on living? What about a starvation that is worse than a lack of food, the disease of loneliness? Or the isolation monster? Even when we feel we have escaped the monster, he can sometimes still re-appear in our mind's eye!

As with our attitude and beliefs, the words we use are determined by, but also a reflection of, what is inside us. The first thing we must do to disempower a fear is to name it. For there will be no movement of our legs if we don't think and say we can overcome our fears and move them.

When a person is struggling with, tempted by, or thinking fearful or negative thoughts, the first thing they must do to address them is name what is causing those thoughts. By saying it aloud, the monsters start to lose their power.

If the thoughts are not named, and crisis strikes, we get caught with unwanted words tumbling out of our mouths. The words express our fears whether we declare, "Peace be still" or we shout out, "We are so toast or done for!" We must explore our connection to, or our relationship with, the dragon.

Defining Connection

A connection is a relationship. It's important to look at defining what relationship means. Google and other sources say a relationship is a fellowship or friendly association, especially with people who share one's interest or a group of people meeting to pursue a shared interest or aim.

The problem with relationships is they can quickly become a swift current in the river. Ideally, we'd like to float on a meandering stream or a lazy portion of the river however, connections tend to rev-up the current to high-speed or even white-water rapids. At times, what we need is a professional guide who has sailed or steered the river before.

The high-speed crashes of relationships in today's social-media-saturated world occur when an individual or a company does something poorly or wrong. Often, the facts do not matter or get lost and, once a story gets started, the speed with which it spreads only increases.

Like the Old West, individuals or organizations may be pursued by a posse that tries, convicts, and lynches them. Once social media gets going, the evidence or investigation of the truth doesn't happen or matter.

A few years ago, videos went viral – before all the facts were known – of a passenger being forcibly escorted off a United Airline flight because of overbooking, causing the airline's stocks to plummet. Many argue that trials are no longer held inside of a courtroom. Instead, they occur in social and other media long before any charges are laid, or a court date is set.

How many of us know of situations where during the time between the social media accusation and the outcome of the trial, the person or organisation has been tried and convicted even though they were innocent?

Healthy connections are no longer assumed, they are choices that must be made. Healthy connections are critical to both resilience and thriving. Why? When the court of public opinion swings, whether about your workplace, your neighbour, your sports team, or the volunteer group you serve with, who will be in your boat?

Sometimes we discover too late that someone is a *frienemy*. Many of us know the sting of being betrayed, the smart from a friend denying they know us, the scar from trusting only to be used, and the sense of shame when people look at us without understanding or compassion. But that reflects on who they are, not us, unless we allow those actions to define you.

So why are connections so important for resilience? Why do relationships and morals matter? What does a healthy connection mean? What do healthy connections look like and how do we obtain them?

So many of our connections have a sense of polite selfishness at their core. We say, "I love you," but sometimes we mean, *I love you because of what you do for me, because you are pretty or handsome, because you are smart,* or *because you are successful.* We may even say, "I love you if (or when) ..." *you meet my needs, you are not too much trouble,* etc.

A connection is a relationship in which a person, thing, or idea is linked or associated with someone or something else. It is a fellowship in which people are connected through companionship or friendly association; a deep connection in which a similar interest, experience, activity, and/or aim exists. A fellowship with a commonality of faithfulness, resilience, and thriving is the strongest and most helpful connection to have.

Today, we live in a time filled with optimism and tolerance, but if you tell someone you don't agree with their values, point of view, thinking, or beliefs, you're told you are wrong or have a phobia. To remain faithful, it is essential to have connections – to have fellowship – with others who do not react to our different values and do not brand us. Instead, they challenge, encourage, and empower us to RTTR. These people will question our values, attitudes, and beliefs but will also get in our boat to row with us, as well.

When feeling lonely, it can feel like no one understands our struggles, and we think we are alone in our turmoil. We cocoon and retreat within ourself. The problem with this is that what we could use is someone to lean on, a connection. We need someone like us to tell us we're not alone. I love the way C.S. Lewis words it in *The Four Loves*, "Friendship is born at the moment when one person says to another, 'What! You, too? I thought I was the only one.'"[77]

Let's return to our monsters. What about the demon of discouragement, the monster of isolation, the beast of betrayal, the leviathan of being villainized, or even the ogre of ostracism? It's quite scary to think about how quickly we adults learn to live with them under our bed. To connect this with our journey, some of the greatest river hazards we will face will be these hidden monsters.

Another monster that rears its head in connections is conflict (or a fear of it).

> *Conflict aversion is the organizational [I would also add individual] bubonic plague of our times. It is cowardice wearing a smart, politically correct hat. The hat allows its entry into all*

human organizations, where it befuddles, ensnarls, and twists communication. It turns dialogue from a leadership tool into a virus to which only a few are immune...it is wrong to adopt fear and avoidance as life principles...we're convinced it would be better to be cowardly than to appear unpopular and alone. Here we are asked to do what appears to be good and assured that doing it is OK if we make a habit of it.[78]

Conflict Resolution

To be a little blunt, conflict resolution never means backing off and giving in. All conflict comes down to two questions:

1. What is the value of the relationship?

2. What is the value of the goal?

It is important to note that within a conflict, each party can be *for* or *against* something but our arguments when we are *against* something are reactive rather than responsive. Conflict in which one argues *for* something requires initiative and energy; it cannot be passive. To be clear, during conflict, we must take a stand for something not against something. It may seem like semantics but, it is more than that, arguing for something is active and positive while arguing against something is reactive and negative. Arguing against something without suggesting an alternative is not helpful. Arguing for something ensures that an alternative to the status-quo or another option exists.

Conflict resolution is never tranquil. This ties into the problem of discipline being confused with punishment. Right now, many abhor discipline and prefer praise, because anything that is not praise is frequently considered punishment.

If you are neutral in situations of injustice, you have chosen the position of the oppressor. If an elephant had its foot on the tail of a mouse and you say you are neutral, the mouse will probably not appreciate your neutrality.

Bishop Desmond Tutu

In the Beatitudes, Jesus says, "Blessed are the peacemakers." Please notice that this does not say peace lovers, peacekeepers, or those who hope for peace! I would never agree that we should *not* want or love peace however we should not seek it at the sacrifice of what we believe is right. There are numerous examples of strong and effective leaders who take time to listen to their hearts and the opinions of others, but they are willing to take a stand and reprimand those who are in the wrong.

That is why for two minutes every November 11th at 11:00 a.m. I and many others pause whatever I am doing and quietly remember those who have laid down their lives for others.

Over and over, people have paid a price for things that we assume are our rights. Ironically, we cannot have rights and freedoms without responsibilities and privileges. One without the other is like all the weight being on one side of a teeter-totter – it simply cannot work!

Today, many simply jettison connections like a tin being recycled. In our hurried existence, people are quick to prescribe solutions to or criticize others' problems or issues, usually from the shore, rather than getting in alongside them in their boat. It might just be my experience, but it seems some people almost find joy in condemning others.

Unhelpful one-liners from those trying to assist in a moment and quick self-righteous counsel from those who feel they have been through it all are all too common. And then there are those who simply say, "I don't need this headache," and delete the relationship like a file on a computer. No remorse. No second-guessing.

Paul wrote a letter saying we must restore the one who was in the wrong.[79] In the original text, before translation, the word restore is a medical term; it refers to a doctor setting a broken arm or *restoring* a broken leg. The idea being that, if it is not restored correctly, the arm or leg will not function properly again. Restoration takes time and care, not a pithy saying or quick judgment.

Taking a Stand

If we continue to avoid conflict rather than stand up for what is right, our inner conflicts tend to grow in discomfort, like a stone in a shoe, as the conflict bubbles up from being left inside for too long.

While we appease another to avoid pain, a refusal to stand up to wrong can result in even more pain and agitation in the relationship. On the other hand, unresolved conflict due to someone standing up for their beliefs (often in anger), without first listening to his or her heart or others' opinions is equally threatening to the connection.

During conflict resolution, it is never a matter of *either/or*; it is *both/and*. There is definitely a time to stand up, but numerous examples demonstrate that it should only come *after* a time of backing down and listening has passed. Resilient people know it is never too late to define a new norm!

Holidays are often disastrous because a common phenomenon occurs between well-acquainted connections from the past. People tend to get frozen in time and are reminded of who they *were*. Family members tend to remember mistakes other members have made, the way they used to react to things, the way they chose to debate topics, and how others responded to them. A margin for change is not granted at these times, but – if we have grown and changed -- it can become an opportunity to create a new norm by responding rather than reacting.

The battle of relationships, morals, and previous painful events is a struggle to achieve transparency, better known as authenticity. When we are authentic, we open ourself up to criticism, judgement, vindictiveness, and anger without any armor to protect us.

There is an old joke that says, *"If it takes six close, personal friends to carry a person from the funeral home to the graveside, many will spend eternity in the funeral home."* Sadly, this is often true – do you have six close, personal friends?

Close connections, or the lack thereof, is highlighted around suicide. The reality is that people under stress know when others truly care – and when they don't. Neuroscience is now proving this biological fact. The connection means that hard questions need to be asked and people must be willing to care enough to ask those questions (and know when to ask them).

The Purdue Social Support Questionnaire (SSQ)[80] measures some core elements each of us needs to have amongst our connections:[81]

- **Emotional Support:** Referring to the provision of support, care, comfort, love, affection, sympathy, and empathy.

- **Encouragement:** Referring to the provision of encouragement, praise, or compliments that demonstrate your importance.

- **Advice:** Referring to the provision of advice, useful information, and help to solve problems.

- **Companionship:** Referring to spending time together, doing things together, visiting each other to demonstrate your value.

- **Tangible Aid:** Referring to the provision of visible assistance with chores or projects, such as babysitting, transportation, money, etc.

- **Overall Helpfulness:** Referring to the provision of general helpfulness when needed.

Search for those who provide one or more of the above elements to you (and, for whom you can supply one or more benefits). The growth achieved by finding these elements for yourself through connections is not always easy or natural to accept, and it is not about a fix. It is about a person listening, hearing, and being present for you.

Toxic Personalities Are Draining

There are toxic personality types that occasionally get entangled in our lives and it's important to identify them to impede their control or influence over us.

- **Manipulative Mary/Mark:** These personalities are manipulation experts; we may not even realize we have been manipulated until it is too late. These individuals figure out our psychological triggers and push them to get what they want. *Why they are toxic:* manipulative personalities have a way of eating away at our belief system and self-esteem. They find ways to get us to do things that we don't necessarily want to do and, before we know it, we lose sense of our identity, our personal priorities, and our ability to see the reality of the situation. The world becomes centred on their needs and their priorities.

- **Narcissistic Nancy/Norm:** These personalities have an extreme sense of self-importance and believe that the world revolves around them. They are often not as sly as the Manipulative Mary/Marks of the world. Instead, they tend to be a bit overt about getting their needs met. We often want to say to them, "It isn't always about you." *Why they are toxic:* Narcissistic personalities are solely focused on their needs, leaving the needs of anyone else in the dust. The connection leaves us disappointed and unfulfilled. Furthermore, by getting us to focus so much on them, we have no energy left for ourselves.

- **Debbie/Donald Downers:** These personalities can't appreciate the positive in life. If we say that it's a beautiful day, they tell us about an impending dreary forecast. If we say that we aced a midterm, they'll tell us about how difficult the final is going to be. *Why they are toxic:* These negative personalities take the joy out of everything. Our rosy outlook on life continues to get squashed with pessimism. Before we know it, their negativity consumes us, and we start looking at things with gray-colored glasses, too.

- **Judgmental Jim/Joanne:** These personalities judge everything and often contrary to us. When we see things as cute and quirky, they see them as strange and unattractive. If we find someone's unique perspectives refreshing, they find it wrong. If we like someone's eclectic taste, they find it disturbing or bad. *Why they are toxic:* Judgmental people are much like Debbie/Donald Downers. Spending a lot of time with these types can unconsciously convert us into a judgmental person, as well.

- **Dream-Killing Karen/Keith:** Every time we have an idea, these personalities tell us why we can't do it. As we achieve, they try to pull us down. As we dream, they are the first to tell us it is impossible. *Why they are toxic:* These people are stuck in *what is* instead of *what could be*. They are unable to dream and are frightened by change. Growth can only occur from doing new things and innovating, never by doing the same things over and over.

- **Insincere Isabel/Ian:** We never quite feel that these personalities are sincere. We tell a funny story, they give us a polite, forced laugh. We feel depressed and sad, and they give us a pat on the arm and a *there-there* response. *Why they are toxic:* Insincere personalities are not genuine and build connections on superficial criteria. This breeds shallow, meaningless relationships. When we are really in need of a friend, they won't be there. Honest feedback will not happen and, when our boat is sinking, they will bail on us –rather than bail the water in the boat!

- **Disrespectful Danny/Donna:** These personalities say or do things at the most inappropriate times and in the most inappropriate ways. They are basically grown-up bullies. *Why they are toxic:* Impertinent personalities have no sense of boundaries and don't respect our thoughts/feelings or our privacy.

- **Never-Enough Neil/Nellie:** These personalities never get enough from us; they always want more. They have unrealistic expectations and take us for granted. They continually find fault and never take responsibility for anything. *Why* *they are toxic:* If we fall under their spell, we spend so much time trying to please them that we end up losing ourselves in the process. They require all our time and energy, so we have nothing left in our own battery, leaving us worn out and our own needs unfulfilled.

Managing connections is challenging at the best of times. Toxic personalities can be particularly harmful. To be resilient and to thrive, we must limit or eliminate toxic types from our connections. Many of us want to help these types but regardless of the way we try to assist them, two things usually happen: firstly, they cannot or are unwilling to see the toxicity they bring into their connections and, secondly, they may weigh us down so that we become toxic, or unhealthy.

To avoid having a toxic personality ourself, we must be willing to ask ourselves how we come across in our connections. If we have a toxic personality, growth and change begin by being completely honest with ourself. What frequently starts a toxicity is some form of a deeply engrained insecurity, which is visible as selfishness, based in our upbringing or a fear. This can be a significant hazard in our river; selfish people do not ask others their opinions or feelings because they do not care. Not listening to and hearing others makes close connections impossible.

A special note, or request, I have to ask that you be *graciously wise when assessing toxicity in others*. Connections must include those who are different but that doesn't mean they are toxic! We all have times when we are unhappy, lonely, stressed, and so on, during which we may come across as toxic. This is *not* toxicity; it is being a typical human.

If the person (or we) is unwilling to do anything about the negative things in her/his life, s/he can grow and become a toxic type. Negative reactions are normal human reactions to things that happen, but left unattended they grow, like a weed, and become toxic. Please practice mercy and, ideally, grace with these people, but buffer the impact and influence they have on your journey.

Recharge With Four Positive Processes

Many training programs and materials highlight four coping mechanisms to support optimism, resilience and thriving. They include:

1. Cognitive reframing,

2. Deep breathing,

3. Goal orientation, and

4. Solution-focused coping.

These four processes help to reorient our cortex so we can remain positive through periods of significant stress; they stop us from reacting rather than responding.

Reorienting the cortex must involve two elements -- reducing our stress reactions and increasing our relaxation. Remember that your autonomic nervous system, which controls involuntary actions like heart rate and digestion, is split into two parts. One part controls the fight--flight-freeze-appease reaction while the other controls our rest and relax response (Chapter Four).

These two parts of the cortex cannot work at the same time, which means if you do things to support one, the other starts to subside. Stress shuts down long-range thinking, including optimism.

When deep breathing is used with cognitive reframing, our reward system is triggered, which produces the hormone dopamine. Dopamine plays a role in feeling pleasure. It's also a big part of our unique, human ability to think and plan. It helps us focus, analyze, and be curious.

Creating Connections

Often, we need to know that our connections reflect our values. They must be based on something more significant than whether we win or lose, have a particular social status, or a certain level of wealth. These qualities of connections are revealed over the long run; values are always costly in the short-term but are beneficial in the long-term.

To feel connected to others, there are three elements required:

1. We must feel content in our own skin,

2. We must have enough satisfactory contact with our close connections.

3. We need to feel connected and feel a sense of belonging to a meaningful group.

Start thinking about other connections as well, whether they be with pets, animals in the wild, nature, plants, other living things, or spiritual entities. A relationship with God or spiritual entity appears particularly important in satisfying those elements.

A relationship with God has been shown to ease the burden of bereavement, divorce, and singlehood. Some studies continue to show the attachment to a group of people who like supportive, interpersonal relationships is beneficial. Lonely individuals who lack close human friendship tend to form the strongest connections to pets. This may be why trauma and service dogs are so incredibly valuable to those who have one.

As well, assessment and constructive criticism is more easily received when it comes from positive connections. Because the connection is close, positive, and value-based, the evaluation ensures that the flaws found are not fatal to the relationship but simply correctable glitches in an otherwise healthy and mutually beneficial connection.

Relationship Management

Relationship management is the act of intentionally managing the types of connections you have in your life, cultivating healthier ones, eliminating toxic ones, examining the frequency of interactions, and establishing the power you allow certain connections to have over you, your decisions, thoughts, and emotions.

Relationship management is required to support healthy bonds and reduce toxic or abusive ones. Some studies have shown that a lack of social connection is a greater detriment to health than obesity, smoking, and high blood pressure. On the other hand, strong social connections lead to a 50% increase in longevity by strengthening the immune system and lowering depression and anxiety.[82] There is also some evidence of higher self-esteem, increased empathy, and increased trust and cooperativeness with others.

A study conducted in the United States regarding social isolation found that the number one determiner in the likelihood of a person to share a personal problem with another was the number of close confidantes a person had; the higher the close connections, the higher the likelihood they would share. [83]

In 1985, individuals, on average, reported having three confidantes; in 2004 this number dropped to one confidante. About 25% of people surveyed in 2004 said that the reason they didn't share personal problems was because they had no one to share them with. With one in four people having no close connections and the two-thirds decrease in confidantes for those that had any, a serious social issue is presenting itself in America.

Discussing the Unthinkable

In our discussion of connections, I would be remiss if I did not raise the topic of suicide. I know this will be uncomfortable for some, so it is important to note that I am not delving deeply into the subject, and this is not a book about diagnosis, research, or other clinical factors regarding suicide.

Many speakers, researchers, and clinicians keep coming back to the connection theme when examining suicide. Obviously, the components of attitudes and beliefs are also involved, but the suicide prevention discussions always return to reaching out, asking for or offering help, and talking with someone. However, when considering suicide, if there is no one to ask for help or to talk to, what can the person unable to see any other solution do?

Suicide frequency is increasing despite mental health being widely discussed publicly and increases in suicide prevention. Why are suicides not decreasing? The logic does not add up. Why is the loneliness of people still extreme and continuing to grow when we can be almost constantly connected through multiple and different platforms?

Are we connecting in the right ways, in circumstances that humans need for meaningful connections? Are we connecting, the right types of relationships so that we can be resilient and thrive?

Despite all the research and marketing about mental/psychological health and safety, there has not been a significant decline in suicides. The opposite is happening. Look at the tug-of-war between increasing positive emotions (and associated behaviors) and the treatment end of the spectrum. On one hand there is love, joy, peace, patience, kindness, gentleness with ourself and with others; on the other, there is an increase in the use of medications, anxiety, depression, stress-related ailments, sickness, substance abuse, etc. These benchmarks represent a barometer of the people who are willing to seek, secure, and receive help.

Suicidal ideations should never be ignored and require common questions to be addressed: Is this normal for you or has a change been slowly taking place? Changes might include alcohol use, irritability, withdrawal, not eating properly, becoming a workaholic, having no balance to life, becoming more impulsive, lack of exercise, experiencing trauma, toxic types, etc.

At the end of the day, suicide is proving to be very difficult to predict.

Communicating on Levels

In the book *Why am I Afraid to Tell You Who I am?*[84] John Powell walks through the different levels of sharing in connections. We vary our sharing based on our level of closeness. Starting with cliché, and moving on through fact, opinion, emotion, and transparency, I have added vulnerability to the bottom of Powell's categories because I believe that it is the deepest level of communication; being vulnerable (sharing what we need) is much riskier than being transparent (sharing who we are) and the number of people we share this type of connection with is few.

We communicate or share different levels with different connections. To be resilient and thrive, we must be willing to grow, to deepen, at least some of our communications to the transparent and vulnerable levels.

Communication Level	Sharing Level	Level of Candour	Number of Connections	Connection Faithfulness
Cliché	Non-Sharing			
Fact	Sharing What I Know			
Opinion	Sharing What I Think			
Emotion	Sharing What I Feel			
Transparent	Sharing Who I Am			
Vulnerable	Sharing What I Need			

Figure 6.1 Levels of Communication
Based on Powell's Levels of Communication, I have added the Vulnerable level, which is the deepest level of communication possible and includes all the levels before it and sharing what we need with one another.

Gary Chapman[86] believes that each of us prefers one main love language *of communication in relationships and at work* (he describes five). He believes most of us have a primary and a secondary love language. If you want to learn more about each love language, give one of his books a read. The one for work is The 5 Languages of Appreciation in the Workplace. It will help make sense of giving and receiving positive love at work, home, or within yourself.

The Four Horsemen of Relationships

Some of the barriers to communication with our connections are quite rudimentary, such as building a willingness to share our thoughts and feelings, difficulty asking close connections for our wants or needs, not understanding how we feel or think, and unhelpful clichés. Other impediments include refusing to discuss issues or problems, using sarcasm or put-downs, and engaging in passive/aggressive instead of an assertive communication style. The most fatal barrier to communication occurs when a person is hearing but is not listening. This state of no communication may be result of constant criticism or pestering.

People become what they are encouraged to become, not what they are nagged to become.

In his book, *The Seven Principles for Making Marriage Work*,[85] John Gottman reveals how he predicts major challenges in relationships due to poor communication strategies. I believe these are vital and valid for any healthy relationship, not just marriages.

Dr. Gottman suggests that "... certain kinds of negativity, if allowed to run rampant, are so lethal to a relationship" that he calls them the Four Horsemen of Relationships (after the Four Horsemen of the Apocalypse). The four fatal negativities are:

- **Criticism:** This involves attacking someone's personality or character rather than a specific behavior. Blame is usually attached to this attack. Criticism is just a step across the line from one of the healthiest things that couples do engage in—complaining (airing anger and disagreement).

- **Contempt:** This involves intentional insults and psychological abuse toward your connection. Common signs include hostile humor, sarcasm, subtle put-downs, and body language such as sneers.

- **Defensiveness:** This is a natural reaction to perceived attack, aggression, or criticism, which can include denying responsibility, making excuses, cross-complaining, whining, and repeating oneself (nagging). In effect, the defensive party is saying, "It's not *my* fault. It's *your* fault!" Defensiveness supports our position at the expense of the other person. When we don't accept any responsibility for our own reactions and actions, the conflict will likely escalate.

- **Stonewalling:** This occurs when we simply refuse to respond (or put up walls). When this becomes a typical pattern, it is destructive because one or both partners are disengaging from any meaningful communication with the other.

Moral Courage

The Institute for Global Ethics was founded in 1990 by Rushworth M. Kidder to promote ethical behavior in individuals, institutions, and nations. Kidder defines moral courage as

> *Standing up for values, the willingness to take a tough stand for right in the face of danger, the courage to do the right thing, the quality of mind and spirit that enables one to face up to the ethical challenges firmly and confidently without flinching or retreating.*[87]

To be faithful, to be resilient, or to thrive comes from living out a values-anchored RTTR ethos.

Thus, we must believe in and commit to a set of morals, values, or guiding principles even though we know that doing so will mean, at some point, facing dangers – our roars. Dangers come in many forms – like monsters under the bed – isolation, being rejected, physical threat, shame, and/or being used by those we trusted.

We must be willing to stay the course because values take years to build but only seconds to lose! We must walk our talk – exhibit the values we believe – to find connections who walk with us.

One of the best examples of a company illustrating both sides of this reality is Johnson & Johnson. In 1982 Johnson & Johnson recalled Extra-Strength Tylenol after seven people died from taking capsules tainted with cyanide. The company offered product replacements for the 264,000 bottles it pulled from shelves, at a total cost of $100 million (to cover the costs of the nationwide recall, the proper cyanide capsule disposal and communication with doctors, consumers and drugstores). But Tylenol's response, which was swift and apologetic, became a business school blueprint for crisis management.

This exact same company has paid billions of dollars involving Johnson & Johnson's baby powder and Shower to Shower products due to cancer causing asbestos being in their products - which they denied. In February 2019, Imerys Talc America, a key talc supplier for Johnson & Johnson, filed for Chapter 11 bankruptcy protection.

While it is easy to be a good person while standing on the shore, watching and telling people what they should do when approaching waterfalls or going through rapids or other hazards in the river, the victory and knowledge of experience belong to those in the river addressing the dangers head-on as they navigate to their destiny and remain faithful. These committed, steadfast people do not change under duress or when roars occur.

When it comes to living with moral courage, acting ethically, living with faithfulness, where are you? On the shore or in the river? If we're to get to our destination, we must be willing and committed to living by the moral code that we have determined for ourselves, regardless of the costs. We must be courageous.

True North and Magnetic North

The world has two Norths:

- True North, or Geographic North, does not move. This marks the northern most point of the earth according to our mapping system of longitude and latitude and is a fixed spot.

- Magnetic North, which marks the spot where the magnetic field, create by the earth's inner activities, points vertically downward. Although geographically close to True North, Magnetic North is in constant motion and moves up to 50 miles (80 km) in a day in a circular motion. This is the point to which our compasses point.

There is always a difference in degrees between the positions of these two points, they are never the same. Our maps are drawn using True North, but our compasses indicate Magnetic North – thus, if we forget to allow for the magnetic differences when calculating our course, we might be heading toward what we think is our destiny, but end up in a very different place. Sometimes a course-correction is in order.

This requires us to look at the true north, not the magnetic north to re-take the bearing for our course. If we do not, the magnetic might draw us off the path we need to be travelling.

To be a person of vulnerability, authenticity, and transparency, we must be willing to look beyond ourselves. Some advocate that selfish people often lose sight of their compass and course because they're always grabbing and taking while rarely giving and serving. Losing sight of our compass and course create the biggest struggles when it comes to being resilient, especially when it comes to targeting our connections.

There are five types of people who lose their compass or stray from their course (or never get on a course):

1. Fakers/pretenders.

2. Spinners or perception designers who can make statistics and figures say whatever they want.

3. Glory hounds who only do something if someone will notice.

4. Loners who try to do everything themselves or don't want to connect with others. and,

5. Magnesium burners who are those who burn brightly, burn brilliantly, but burn quickly – they are the shooting stars in the sky.

It is very easy to live by our values when times are good. Some believe that is the biggest hurdle for some societies – it has been good for so long that we don't know what it's really like to be under pressure.

Two questions at the time of roars help determine if we will forget our compass, course, or destiny:

- What is most of value, most important, to you?

- Will this (roar) matter in 15 minutes or 5 days (as that will impact our choices in the long run)?

It is very easy to drift into hazards or an eddy if we are not focussed on our destiny, true north. They say hindsight is 20/20, but this is a lie that many people have been telling themselves for years. Because we now know things that we did not know at the time, it is *not* hindsight but completely new knowledge.

Connecting to Our Social Support

Repeatedly, one of the greatest values that comes out of a small group model is a sense of support, the knowledge that others are willing to get in the boat with you, even when it feels like it's sinking, rather than stand on the shore and shout at us to paddle harder.

Numerous people have studied the importance of social ties and social support systems in relationships to mortality and disease rates. One of them, Leonard Syme, a professor of Epidemiology at the University of California at Berkeley. He points to Japan as being the number one country in the world regarding health. He cites the close social, cultural, and traditional ties in that country as the reason. Syme believes that the more social connections a person has, the better health and longevity they will have. Conversely, he specifies that the more isolated a person is, the poorer their health and the sooner their death. Social ties are good preventative measures for physical, mental, emotional, and behavioural problems. [88]

Living according to our values and faith must permeate all areas of our life. They cannot be siloed and remembered only periodically. There are always two sets of values in play: the actual values and the aspirational values. The actual values are the ones we live on a daily basis. These actual values are where we spend our time and our money. When the pressure is on, when a roar is heard, it is the actual morals and values that will leak out (remember the Tea-Bag Effect, Chapter Three). The aspirational values are ones we tell people, the ones we want to be known by, but not actually living on a daily basis.

Siloed values that are not practiced every day in every area of our life will not be the ones that we display during stress. Only those we follow daily – whether positive or negative – will be leaked and displayed when we hear a roar. If our values encourage us to face the roar and run toward it, we will be resilient and will survive; if we choose any other response, we will survive but may never rebound or be the same again.

Connecting To Our Core Values

Core values are motivational preferences, not just ethics. They are not just basic or operational.

Ethics can be determined by the mirror test: What kind of person do I want to see in the mirror in the morning?

Values are motivational preferences or choices, which consistently characterize our behaviors or that of a group, a non-profit, or any other organization or workplace. They may be carefully considered or simply spontaneous. These core values are more than goals or ideals. They are choices and preferences that require a continual commitment. Values are the behaviors that encapsulate a person, business or organization, character, and culture.

Why not draw a line in wet concrete rather than sand?

Oscar Wilde once said, "Morality, like art, means drawing a line someplace." I want to ask you to think about my next questions, as they relate to values. Why is it that people say draw a line in the sand? After all, if we draw a line in the sand, a strong wave, wind, or any number of other things can move and erase it. That way, when it sets, it is a line that people can see, count on, and we can make a commitment not to cross it.

These core values supply meaning to our life and work because they influence our decisions. Our values compel us to take a stand at those times when a no or yes is simply non-negotiable. They set an atmosphere in which we are the most productive and they determine where we choose to draw a line in the wet concrete.

Let me illustrate with a personal story. We had our taxes prepared and it was revealed that I owed several thousand dollars! As you can imagine this created a crisis reaction during which I wondered how we would come up with those funds. I went into meet the accountant and sign the paperwork and explained my shock. The accountant said she could put some of the income under my wife's return and see if that made a difference. I agreed and asked her to try. The difference amounted to a couple hundred dollars, so I said, "Never mind."

After I left, I called her back and said, "I didn't ask what your thoughts are on my decision, and tax is your area of expertise." She laughed and said she agreed with my decision as a few hundred dollars was not worth the potential risk, and then she added, "But John, this is more of a moral issue than a tax issue." Imagine her description of me and my morals if I had said yes!

Some of these core values, or virtues, will change depending on our current stage of life. For example, young families may have a higher core value of family than an empty nester or retired person, but they may have a similar definition as to what a core value of family looks like. We also must be willing to have a written definition of our own core values because when the heat is on, there must be something in writing to which we are committed. These values must be able to be defined and easily measured using SMART goals (see Chapter Two). Again, like many things in life, if it is not in writing then it does not exist!

Teaching Our Values

If we do not have definitions in writing of these core values, it will be impossible to teach or discuss with others what we mean. When verbalized, confusion between what others think we mean and what we actually mean often occur. Without a written version of our values burned in our brain, our teachings or discussion could diverge from our definition, and we could end up being branded as a hypocrite or judgemental.

When values clash, we must be willing to practice what we preach. We must be able to follow our values beyond the good times and we must be willing to live out these values fully. We all display our values without words, and they are reflected in how people describe us (non-physically), etc.

A relationship starts with the question *who is it I want to connect with?* It is about empathy not sympathy, listening not just hearing, asking what I can do to improve or help, giving feedback, and self-disclosure.

I want to add a note here about natures, or personalities. Failure to finish a task does not always mean that a person is uncaring. Similarly, a person with a nature or personality that has a need to finish tasks does not indicate that person is controlling. Sometimes different personalities do not need to finish everything they start while others do.

Solomon said that we are to "train up a child in the way he should go; even when he is old, he will not depart from it."[89] This does not mean rules and punishment should prevail but that we help a child learn how s/he is wired so that s/he can live out her/his life with her/his wiring successfully (by whatever definition of success s/he chooses).

Here is a simple truth, that Josh McDowell shared in a KLTV interview,

> *Parents, first of all, need to know one thing: Truth without relationships leads to rejection, rules without relationships lead to rebellion, discipline without relationship leads to bitterness, anger and resentment. It's the relationship, Stupid, it's the relationship.*[90]

That is foundational for all connections, whether parenting, in the workplace, on a sports team, in a friendship, with our neighbor, and with anyone we meet. It is especially true when a friend or loved one is trying to tell us about behaviors we display but do not see or want to see.

Moral Injury

When it comes to dealing with first responders, veterans, ER staff, and others in similar roles, there is a lot of talk of *moral injury*. The concept of moral injury emphasizes the psychological, social, cultural, and spiritual aspects of trauma. Distinct from psychopathology, moral injury can be a normal human reaction to a significantly abnormal traumatic event.

Moral injury occurs when a person is ordered to do something in a situation that violates her/his deeply held beliefs about what is right or wrong. The symptoms of moral injury are very similar to a person dealing with traumatic stress and include depression, anxiety, numbness, irritability, feeling out of control, and avoidance.

A great movie that raises this theme of moral injury, but also the beliefs and relationship themes, was *Hacksaw Ridge*. It is based on the true story of a US soldier whose beliefs did not allow him to bear arms – however, he wanted to be a soldier.

Google has dealt with this moral injury discussion. There was an uprising by some of their employees when they were building Artificial Intelligence (AI) because they knew it would be used for a military drone program. The result was a petition demanding a clear policy stating that neither Google nor its contractors will ever build warfare technology.

This is happening right now in many environments. There are many names for what is occurring: harassment, racism, bullying, disrespect, lateral violence, toxicity, etc. The bottom line is that these unhealthy, demoralizing environments exist.

What we permit, we promote!

When it comes to psychological health and safety, we must be very clear about moral injury and what price are we willing to pay if something is happening that we cannot live with. To be resilient and to thrive requires us to RTTR rather than simply react to life and events.

It is vital for us to define our norm and believe that we cannot cross our line in the concrete. In the workplace, for others to assume responsibility for what our values should be is morally wrong. Dealing with this tension will mean conflict, and sometimes the other party is not the one who must change.

Forgiveness

Any discussion about connections and values must include the topic of forgiveness.

First, let me be crystal clear – forgiveness does not mean, imply, or suggest that we forget or condone what has happened. We are not skipping over the consequences of what happened, and we're not pretending that a relationship will be restored depending upon what has happened. We can forgive a person while at the same time believe that their actions and/or behaviors where morally wrong.

Accepting an apology is not necessarily forgiveness. Sometimes, forgiveness can happen without ever speaking to or interacting with the person who did us wrong. Forgiveness is a conscious act by the one wronged. To forgive, we must make a conscious decision to let go of the wrong that has happened to us. Payback (or revenge) is not our goal, and we must choose to let go of our resentment, anger, or other emotions around this issue even if they might be very reasonable feelings.

Forgiveness involves practicing grace toward the offender (see Chapter Five). When people tell me, "I just can't forgive," the first thing that we have to talk about is what forgiveness means because often the people who can't forgive think forgiving is forgetting. This is simply not true.

A second misunderstanding about forgiveness is that we have to trust the person who hurt us again. There is a vast difference between forgiving and trusting someone. I believe that trust is a performance issue and is about commitments and deliverables. If we make a commitment and we do not deliver on it, trust erodes; if we make a commitment and over deliver, trust grows. Forgiveness is possible without the restoration of trust in the one who wronged us.

Be aware that commitments are determined by the person listening, *not* by the person who has spoken. In other words, communication is never about what was said but always about what was heard. When it comes to forgiveness and trust, forgiveness is something we can (and should, for our own sake) do almost immediately, while trust is something that can only be built up over time, or possibly rebuilt if trust has been broken.

Connection Challenges

There is a whole host of connection challenges, and any connection may be affected by one or more challenges, almost daily. Let's briefly review some common examples.

Stress

Stress itself is neutral as it will depend on what type of stress it is (see Chapter Four). Some stress is positive and challenges us to do our best, while other stressors are negative. When stressed, we tend to get upset over small things that would not normally irritate us; things get blown out of proportion and may result in an argument.

Finding time is not possible. We either take it or it passes by!

Time Balancing

Balancing our time is related to the bigger subject of finding balance. As time is a commodity (once spent, it can never be recovered), it requires a decision beforehand that many of us do not make. Connections require time to nurture and grow – connections do not survive if we do not make time for them.

Differing Beliefs

A challenge with huge energy behind it will be working through differing beliefs. Be sure to watch this one when it comes to roles in the home, parenting, work activities, etc. Differing beliefs can also manifest as budget or financial management differences, household chore disputes and different opinions about individual responsibilities, toys that are bought, trip decisions, career aspirations, etc.

Intimacy And Communication

Intimacy includes not only the sexual intimacy between people but also emotional, experiential, spiritual, intellectual, creative, and communication intimacy. Intimacies can be one of the most rewarding and fulfilling elements of connections.

However, closeness and devotion, or lack thereof, can also be the source of hurt, rejection, upset, or embarrassment. Please note that I am referencing sharing at the deeper levels of transparency and vulnerability (see Figure 6.1).

There are a host of concerns that may arise within a connection, but one thing that seems to be common among many relationships, including couples or parenting, is that when there is difficulty at the vulnerability and transparency levels, there are often stresses in the connection at other levels, as well.

Let me give you a glimpse into the reason why. When a positive, confident connection exists between two people, it spawns a genuine closeness. This closeness and our positive feelings build trust and allow both people to be more open and able to deal with issues that arise in other areas. When these goes awry at the highest communication levels, everything else seems more difficult, too. It is very tough to deal with a deep hurt with someone who only wants to talk about the weather and last night's game.

Most of us realize that effective communication is key to any successful connection, but many of us are challenged to put this understanding into practice. Sometimes we may lack the skill; sometimes we allow anger to override our skills. One thing is certain – the foundation of good communication is our delivery. Over time, couples may find that their patience and the respective communication style they used during the initial stage of the connection disintegrates into hostility and negativity if they do not continue to work on their communication skills.

Connection Corrections

What does this all mean for our connections? It means we must create a new set of behaviors or truisms that support mental health and resilience within our communities, workplaces, and in our own life.

Part of being resilient and being able to thrive through crisis by running toward the roar involves addressing joy stealers and troublemakers. Look at your workplace. Who charges your battery or makes an investment in you? Are you spending enough time with them to gain the benefits of your connection?

The question is asked,

> *Is there anything more beautiful in life than a boy and a girl*
> *clasping clean hands and a pure heart in the path of marriage?*
> *Can there be anything more beautiful than young love?*

And the answer is given,

> *Yes, there is a more beautiful thing. It is the spectacle of an old man and an old woman finishing their journey together on that path. Their hands are gnarled, but still clasped; their faces seamed, but still radiant; their hearts physically bowed and tired, but still strong with love and devotion for one another. Yes, there is a more beautiful thing than young love. Old love.*

Author unknown

People Needed for the Journey

Finally (but not lastly), there are some professionals you will need or want to connect with to assist you during parts, or all, of your journey:

- **Therapists:** Like the boat mechanic or other expert on ensuring the boat operates properly, therapy can act as insurance for our lives. Therapy focuses on resolving difficulties arising from the past that hamper an individual's functioning in the present, improving overall psychological functioning, and dealing with the present in more emotionally healthy ways. The mechanic addresses the issues that hinder our boat from working at its best and most capable, as does a therapist.

- **Consultants:** Individuals or organizations retain consultants for their expertise. We call consultants to learn how to travel in our boat. The ones who can identify why we keep going right when we wanted to go straight or why we keep drifting even though we've dropped anchor. They will identify problems, potential solutions, and, if needed, are able to implement solutions.

- **Mentors:** Mentors started on their journey before us; they've been there and done that. S/he is still on her/his journey, yes, but s/he has been on it longer than us and had more experience and practice with the ABCs, refining norms, facing roars, finding her/his course and destiny. S/he provides wisdom and guidance based on experience.

- **Trainers/Coaches:** Trainers and coaches teach lessons that we take before we think we can navigate the waterways without going over the falls! This will tend to be a set process that we need to learn, then move through, until we have the confidence to go on our own. Note that trainers and coaches may also be helpful if you become overwhelmed or fallback in your practice of running toward the roar and need a refresher.

- **Peer Supporters:** As the name suggests, these are others in the river around you, they are going through similar challenges and hazards and are also struggling (or cruising) on their own course – they are your peers. and have made the same amount of progress along their journey. These are the people who will come alongside you, who will help when you need support, and who you will help when they need assistance.

The ultimate measure of a man is not where he stands in moments of comfort and convenience, but where he stands at the times of challenge and controversy.... Cowardice asks the question: is it safe? Expediency asks the question: is it politic? Vanity asks the question: is it popular? But conscience asks the question: is it right? And there comes a time when one must take a position that is neither safe, nor politic, nor popular – but one must take it simply because it is right.

Martin Luther King, Jr.

The coaching I love to be part of for others as they define their new norm involves asking questions but – instead of analyzing problems or the classic, "Why did you do that? Why did that happen?" approach – I focus on creating solutions. It is not a one-size-fits-all process. We must be willing to think about our individual thinking and to define our individual new norm so that it is not defined by life or others.

Of course, there are exceptions to the list above and we may have more than one of any type of professional connections along our journey, but – usually – there are *three VERI connections* in our life to whom we need to be *accountable*:

1. A person who is more mature than us, who we want to emulate or learn from.

2. A person who is less mature than us, into whom we can become invested (we learn something best by teaching others).

3. A person who is a positive observer. Someone who wants us to succeed but cares enough to question what they see and challenge us to think about what we are doing. While some may always tell us we can leap a tall building in a single bound and others think we are a fool, observers care enough to ask why you do something without loading you with false praise or extreme criticism for your answer.

These people are not simply going to slap our hand when we do something wrong or don't do it at all; they are the ones who *encourage* us to keep trying, even when we feel like tapping out.

PART III

A Life (And Book) Examined

This brief, final section is to warn you of some things you may face. If doing the things outlined in *Run Toward the Roar* were simple, then everyone would be thriving and there would be no reason to discuss succumbing, surviving, and resilience.

We have walked through many factors that impact your resilience and your opportunity to thrive. We have discussed being reactive, like a normal human being, and choosing to proactively respond to roars. We have walked through building an ethos in which you define and refine a new norm and choosing a destiny you value. When your values are clear, and you have learned your ABCs, you/we can grow toward your destiny. When roars knock you off course, you can find the way to get back on course.

In this final section of the book, we will look at using what we have learned in real life, which always seems to show up in unique situations and issues. We will discuss the intrarelationship between the ABCs and its importance to growing forward and focus on our destiny – even when we get off-course. We will look at the positives of crises – and how easily these can slide into The Eddy Effect when we fail to recognize the difference between *urgent* and *important*. We will examine the dangers of drift, the time we need to be ready to spend on RTTR, and the struggle with decisions. We will learn lessons from lobsters and the importance of examining our life and reflecting on what we see.

Imagine how incredible it would be if we could thrive only by eating properly or only by showing our emotions when appropriate. Wouldn't it be incredible if we could just think positive thoughts and thriving would come easily? Paramount to this section is the commitment you must make and time it will take to develop a RTTR ethos.

From time to time I work with individuals and couples, outside of my corporate work. I remember working with a first-responder couple who were sharing the things that were draining their battery before they even managed to be with their children each day. Everyone else's demands were so huge while their own destiny, and their ABCs, were not clear.

Every roar (which occurred daily) resulted in them bouncing in another direction. Their work repeatedly drew them into eddy after eddy and they lost sight of their destiny. It was affecting their faithfulness to one another, their family, and themselves. They wanted to know what they could do to fix what was happening. We talked about drifting off course and the effort needed to get back on track. They walked away for at least six months and then came back. However, their commitment to doing the work was not any stronger than it was when we first met, so they were still in the same place – their giant eddy – they needed to commit to changing, to growing, to have success.

I can verify that procrastination will not take you in the direction you want to go. I have tried it, seen it tried by others, and it does not work.

Remember, your values are what seep out when you are in the hot water or in a roar, whether they are good, bad, better, or great. Choose them carefully and then commit to them, practice them in good times so that in bad times you remain faithful to them and can stay your course.

This change will involve growth. Indeed, all the changes suggested in this book involve growing forward. But growth is never comfortable, because it requires change, taking risks, and consistency; it can be scary. It might feel safer to resist change and growth, but the long-term costs of doing so are always higher than any risk associated with growth.

Have you ever started something only to discover that it feels like you've been cheated? Those moments when we trust and get burned?

I want to be completely transparent about what you are getting into. Is it worth it? Without exception or reservation, 100%, yes. But do not think you can RTTR and finish well without discipline, effort (work), or support.

A crisis is a

terrible thing.

But a

crisis is

also a terrible thing

to waste!

CHAPTER SEVEN

Lobster Lessons and Life Examined

When my wife and I were first married, we lived in Cape Breton, Nova Scotia. We loved many things about the Maritimes, but I always felt bad about the life of lobsters on the island. Despite the disbelief of other diners, I was never able to finish eating one of those creatures, despite the delicious flavor everyone claimed they had. For me, the flavor was literally nauseating.

Lobster Lessons

The first lobster lesson I learned was that just because most people value something and seek it out does not mean that all people have the same values. Although I love watching people thoroughly enjoy their lobster, I have absolutely no desire to eat one myself. My system and lobster just do not mix well. This does not mean that one is wrong and the other right, it simply means that sometimes people have different values, but our time together can still be enjoyed.

Like all exoskeletal creatures, lobsters molt to grow. When molting, lobsters are highly vulnerable to prey and other hazards that can kill them without their hard shell. Thus, lobsters behave differently during molts to protect themselves. They tend to hide with their mates and other lobster in caves and safe locations in rocks and reefs until their new shell has hardened.

The second lesson I learned from lobsters is that when vulnerable, we must surround ourselves with those who will protect us, and we also must be self-preserving and take cover until we are ready to take on the world and challenges again. There will be seasons for growth during which -- whether dealing with fears, anger, grief, an emergency, addiction, or a variety of other challenges – we must face roars through self-evaluation, receiving feedback, criticism, encouragement, and the differing perspectives of others to grow.

The fishing season for lobster in Atlantic Canada is limited to ensure the specie's survival, which is part of the reason that no fishing is allowed during the molting season. When it is open season, fishers catch lobsters using traps (pots), into which the lobsters are drawn with bait. The pot has a kitchen into which the bait is placed and a parlour into which the lobsters crawl and are trapped.

The third lobster lesson is that there are seasons for growth and seasons for reflection. There are times when we get drawn into traps by the bait in the kitchen and it will be hungers that can draw us away from our destiny. The hungers occur in eddies where we get a taste of something we want more of – status, power, money, possessions, relationships, etc. We must accept that there are times when different connections, or times when we need to just be alone. Running toward the roar and thriving or being resilient cannot always be worked at. Sometimes it is life-giving to pause and just look at what you have already accomplished and how far you have travelled.

When lobsters are being cooked some say they squeal or scream. Since they do not have any vocal cords, this is not possible. The squealing/screaming is caused by air or vaporized water escaping from their shells.

This fourth lobster lesson recalls our lesson about being in hot water and the Hot-Water-Tea-Bag Principle: Yes, when in hot water, what's inside will leak out but, as we RTTR, when it feels like the air is being squeezed out of us, we will be able to press on. With the right values, attitudes, beliefs, and connections, we'll create a new norm, adjust our course, keep an eye on our destiny, avoid eddies, and continue our journey without a detour.

I do not believe anyone plans to drift off course, but it still happens to many of us. It's during times of growth, when we shed the outer protection, or times when we just pause without any pressures that we can revisit our focus and what we are being faithful to as we RTTR.

Life Examined

Socrates said, *"The unexamined life is not worth the living."*[91] Indeed, we learn nothing and remain unchanged if we do not reflect on our actions, reactions, behaviors, responses, and choices.

Reviewing psychological research and other sources shows that some of our poorer decisions are instinctive, or reactive, rather than reflective, or responsive. To be responsive, we must determine the values to which we will remain faithful and adopt them into our attitudes, beliefs, and connections, so when roars occur and hazards appear, we are resilient and thrive because we've examined, questioned, and defined our norm so we can RTTR.

Within this book and the *RTTR Discovery Guide*, I've attempted to lead you on an interactive journey in which we explore the way you think, feel, and react. I've also challenged you to question your own motivations, beliefs, principles, preferences, and values to provide the tools you need to strengthen your resiliency for improved success all areas of your life.

Run Toward the Roar does not work well as a *shelf-help* book. It requires work and requires you to open the *Discovery Guide* and your journal, look deep within, look around, and take inventory of all with as much integrity, compassion, and faith as you have. There is also a growing library of additional resources that you can access online at: runtowardtheroar.online/resources.

Working through this book is not a once-and-done exercise. Rather, it is a life-long practice, I believe that living happens while in your boat on the river, guided by your new norms toward your destiny; you are not fully living when you are drifting or onshore watching others. The information, questions, and journal topics I have laid out are designed to be evergreen; they will last your lifetime and serve as lifelong practices to help you continue your quest to thrive.

What may be most amazing is how your answers and journal entries will change over the years as your resiliency grows. I recommend revisiting *Run Toward the Roar* and the *RTTR Discovery Guide* every year to re-examine your own state, note your growth, and continue to work the areas that matter to you, your relationships, and your work.

A Few Cautions

I want to be sure you RTTR with your eyes wide open.

The warning for you is to please be very careful. There will be some hazards that may capsize you despite your best efforts; there will be places on the river which seem good to stop; and, while working with the ABCs, we can get off course quickly even with good intentions.

I offer the following topics only as some areas to be cautious:

- The Intrarelationships Of Thriving
- The Upside Of Crisis
- The Subtlety Of Drift
- Time Is Required
- Decisions, Whether You Like It Or Not

The Intrarelationships Of Thriving

Let's look at the word resilience. It comes from the Latin word *resilio*, which means to bounce back, to spring forward, or rebound. In our context, however, I do not want anyone to bounce backward. Ideally, we want to move forward or rebound to the same place. To do so, the core of your relational elements will need to develop, strengthen, and be reinforced by refining your new norm and destiny so you can thrive.

Figure 7.1 illustrates what I am talking about. If we think about our being as composed of our values, to which we are faithful and, thus, which influence our behaviors. The core of our being is our A, B, and Cs. To travel forward – toward our destiny – through ups and downs (or roars), our core – the ABCs – must be balanced and strong to bounce – or be resilient.

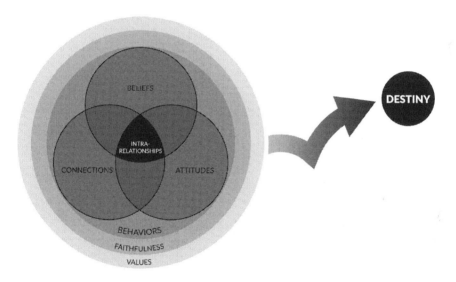

Figure 7.1 The Relationship of All We've Examined.
This figure depicts the relationship between our values, faith, behaviors, ABCs, our path, and our destiny. To be able to respond to roars (bounce) and remain on course to our destiny, our core must be balanced and strong. Thus, the ABCs must be equally strong and couched within our values, faith, and behaviors.

Where the ABCs overlap, in the intrarelationships between these elements, determines our direction when we face a roar. If there is imbalance, it is essential for us to admit and address that imbalance.

If we try to move forward with a strong Attitude without having Beliefs and/or Connections of the same strength, our core will be out of

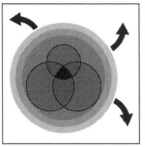 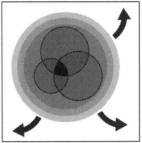 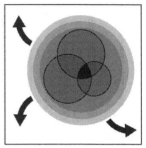

Figure 7.2 The Results Of An Imbalance Between the ABCs.
If any one of our Attitudes, Beliefs, or Connections are weaker or stronger than the other two, our ability to travel where we want to go is impeded.

balance. Although we may have resilience (that is, we bounce), we will probably not bounce in the direction of our destiny, and it is unlikely we will thrive.

As well, to ensure that our behaviors are maintained, our core – the intrarelationships between the ABCs – must remain strong and balanced. We must consistently watch the intrarelationships so one core area does not become so soft or weak that we cannot be faithful and honor our values.

We grow toward our destiny when our ABCs are all healthy and strong; then we can bounce in the right direction, and not merely react or bounce all over the place. If we do not, then our values and our desire to be faithful will be challenged and it will not be possible to bounce in the direction to which we are committed.

This principle is true for so many areas that require the bounce principle to play the game – whether it is the golf ball meeting the club or a baseball meeting a bat – when life gives us the roars, to be able to bounce and RTTR, our values and faithfulness will only be as sound as our ABCs and their intrarelationship.

The Upside Of Crisis

Please do not pretend or believe that this journey toward a new norm will be smooth or easy. Yes, it sounds simple – rather than reacting to roars, choose your response and run toward them – but, perhaps, that is the issue with it.

We have this tendency to want immediate gratification. We love the quick or simple fixes. We focus on the next hazard and then move to address it, without creating a long-range strategy. Even our health-care system is designed to care for the sick rather than prevent illness to begin with. A take-this-pill-twice-a-day strategy rather than an eat-in-moderation-and-exercise strategy to stop the illness before it happens.

The upside to crisis is that it gives us something to focus on for the next period. After all, current thinking for many is that if it is marked "urgent," it must be important – which often is not true. Urgent does not mean important. But turning urgent things into crises makes us pay attention and deal with them, even if they do not deserve prioritized attention.

Look at the use of the word *busy*. Sometimes, saying one is busy can quickly become a badge of honour – it means you are dealing with crises (even though you may not be, in your mind you are).

Busy does not always mean important.

Do you need proof? Ask someone if they are busy, and most people say, "Yes." Ask them if they are occupied, and most will look at you funny. The next time you are asked if you are busy, think before you respond. "No, not really. My schedule is full, but I am not busy," Is a valid response. But there will often be the sound of crickets after it -- what do you mean you are not busy?! These descriptors reflect different qualities: *Busy* is often driven by someone else's schedule while *full* is driven by your priorities and schedule.

So yes, there is an upside to treating everything as a crisis and being busy. If we are always *busy*, we do not have time to think about resilience or defining our new norm because we are so busy just surviving. Alternatively, if we revise our thinking and our language, and are willing to have a full schedule with which we are occupied, then resilience and thriving can be ours by choice!

Crisis can work like a slap across the face, a kick in the butt, or a roar to wake us up from our daydream. If we are not careful, we can make decisions in a fog without long-range thinking and end up worse off. When life roars and we are awakened, we must pause and look around to see where we are, think about where we truly want to go, and start paddling in that direction.

This change feels like various therapies (e.g., physiotherapy, massage therapy, etc.). There will usually be some discomfort (if not outright pain). Like physiotherapy, sometimes thinking (or working) in a different way will cause us discomfort, but if we want to improve how we function, we must continue with the personal practices.

The Subtlety Of Drift

When it comes to making the decision to grow, it's vital not to be lulled into hoping, wishing, or praying for change to happen. If you do nothing or are happy with the status quo, you have made a choice. Despite hoping, wishing, or praying for change, the willpower will not exist to start the change(s). Watch what happens when we decide that something needs to get done!

Our willpower is directly influenced by our ABCs of resilience and thriving. If we do not choose to think about our thinking, if we do not choose our attitude so our behaviors and emotions follow, if we do not define our beliefs, morals, and what spirituality means for us, if we do not decide what a great relationship means in our lives, then there is nothing steering our boat and we will drift along and be thrown about by the currents, buoys (fears), and hazards (crises) within the river. We cannot will our boat to go the way we want it to without changing our ABCs; it has a sail, paddle, motor, keel, and rudder, but there is no course set and nothing steering it.

Without any course or steering, our emotions steer the boat. Then our course is set by our urges rather than our VERI PLAN. Because we are thinking, social animals, the next factor that starts to steer our boat is peer pressure and competition, keeping up with the Jones will dominate our purpose as wants become needs.

The person who is perfectly content and wants for nothing cannot be sold anything. The only appeal that reaches people in that position is one asking for service to others – altruism. Most people do not reach that place until crisis happens and their actual needs are laid starkly out before them. If the crisis acts as a catalyst for growth, then a new norm can be developed, and values with long-term expression emerge. The tyranny of the urgent fades.

Drifting results in a gradual shift in position; an aimless course; to become carried along subject to no guidance or control. Boats may be drifting because of poor guidance or steering, lack of fuel, lack of wind for the sails, etc., but most often drifting happens for one reason – neglect. Crises of significant change can grab our attention and make clear the need to steer a drifting boat.

> *Blessed is the one who finds wisdom, the one who gains understanding ...*[92]

> *Wisdom is supreme; therefore, get wisdom. Though it cost you all you have, get understanding.*[93]

Often, we stop steering when things get tough in life, rather than staying the course. What makes drifting so perilous is that it is so very easy to fall into. All a person must do to drift is nothing. Drifting requires no effort. Staying the course, on the other hand, requires enormous energy, which requires more than good intentions and hopeful thinking. It requires a power source and commitment. No one ever drifts toward a positive and refined new norm; they drift away from that.

History is full of examples of those who started out strong but drifted toward their end, becoming spiritually weak, compromising when it came to long-term values, falling in love with the things of the world, or drifting away from those relationships who believed in them and spoke the truth to them when they needed it.

There are signals warning of drift that I have learned over the years (often the hard way). For example, impulse, or seat-of-the-pants, living leads to drifting quicker than others. I am listing some signs of drift for your contemplation and not to prescribe anything, except caution.

If you want to be resilient through crisis/change, encourage others toward resilience, and live out your new norm and watch out for the following:

Failure To Pay Attention to Truths

Think about training, conferences, or events you have been at where they provide you with a hearty lunch. I hate training, or anything that requires focus, right after those large lunches because I am drowsy and can easily drift. It is not only food that can cause a lack of attention: monotony, distractions, other people, assumptions (I know what you are going to say or do), and many other shiny objects can cause us to fail to pay attention to what we should.

Continuous Partial Attention (CPA), as described by Linda Stone[94], means paying partial attention to everything continuously. It involves trying to pay attention to everything a bit, but nothing in depth. Its purpose is to connect and be connected, always scanning for an opportunity and optimizing to get the best opportunities, activities, and contacts in any given moment. The goal is to be busy, be connected, feel alive, be recognized, and matter.

We use CPA to address our FOMO (see Chapter One). If we are always aware – anywhere, anytime, anyplace – we won't miss anything we don't want to. The problem is that CPA creates a sense of constant crisis. We are always on high alert when we practice CPA. This artificial sense of constant crisis is more typical of CPA than multi-tasking because when multi-tasking we have a finite, pre-determined (often self-chosen) set of things demanding our attention while CPA requires us to notice everything and evaluate its value to us as we go through our day.

In a time when more people would rather be infatuated by games and trivialities than reality or truth, we are practicing CPA non-stop. We are consistently on high alert.

The result is that if the truth is not external for us, we tend to live according to the truth we feel at any moment, but since feelings can change from moment to moment, that means we lose sight of the truth.

Forgetting Basic Truths

If I had a quarter for every time I heard the claim, "People lack common sense today," I would be a millionaire.

The principles of both the Universal Law of Cause and Effect – in which every cause has an effect, and every effect has a cause – and Newton's Law of Action-Reaction – in which every action has an equal and opposite reaction – apply here. Common sense grows out of seeing the consequences of one's actions according to the truth. However, if the truth is that there are no consequences for what we do, then we cannot develop common sense, as that requires a truth with consequences.

Some peoples' responses during the COVID-19 pandemic illustrate this premise. Some acted and behaved like the virus was not a big concern and continued with their regular activities and refused to wear masks, without any concern about the consequences for those they might infect or the consequence of getting sick themselves. Rather than there being no truth in this case, the truth was that unprotected and without social distancing, people became ill, not to mention the consequences to the healthy system and personnel.

To have common sense, one must have experienced consequences, and consequences are based in truths.

Sitting Unanchored

We must be careful when we want to rest or sleep while on our journey. We must be sure to anchor our vessel. When we rest, we are not looking out around us and we are also out of others' eyeline. If we do not anchor, we can end up heading right toward a hazard (or have one heading toward us). The river changes as does life; things will happen while we are sleeping, and we can find ourselves carried off by currents or hazards.

Failure To Practice and Reinforce

If we don't continue to apply and reinforce what we learn, have we really learned anything? How many times have we learned something, been tested on what we learned, and then cannot recall anything that we'd learned when asked about it the following year? To continue to grow, be resilient, and thrive, we must continue practicing and reinforcing our RTTR ABCs and refining our new norm.

Becoming Prone To Peril On The Waterway

There is the tide of years and time. Think of the number of marriages that started out filled with love and companionship that have drifted, career paths that were so hopeful, relationships with friends, God, or even values. Suddenly, or over time, they are not on the radar anymore.

There is also the tide of familiarity with the truth. It is so easy for the familiar, the most often repeated and heard, to become merely commonplace. Familiarity can breed contempt. There is the hazard of busy-ness mentioned earlier, too. There is the hazard of lip service (or lip-sync). There are those seasons when we are simply going through the motions.

Please be aware and cautious about some perils of drifting:

- Without paddles, sails, or a keel, we know we will begin to drift. But drifting can also start unconsciously. Whether it is undercurrents in the water, wind we don't feel, the compass versus a bearing of True North, or even the rudder not being at a perfect 90° angle, we will not go where we want to if we do not have something helping us get there.

- We will never drift against the river's current; we certainly never drift upstream. If we want to live out our VERI PLAN (see Chapter Three), we cannot just go with the flow. The going-with-the-flow approach also picks up its own speed. It has been said many times, going with the flow means travelling toward waterfalls and by the time we hear the waterfalls, it is too late.

Time Is Required

There's an old legend about three men crossing a desert on horseback at night. As they approach a dry creek bed, they hear a voice commanding them to dismount, pick up some pebbles, put them in their pockets, and not look at them until the next morning. The men are promised that if they obey, they will be both glad and sad. After they do as they were told, the three mount their horses and carry on their way.

As the first streaks of dawn began to spread across the sky, the men reach in their pockets and pull out the pebbles. To their great surprise, they had picked up diamonds, rubies, and other precious gems. It is then that they realize the significance of the promise that they would be both glad and sad: They are happy they had picked up as many pebbles as they did but are sad – so sad – that that they didn't collect more.

As you journey along the river and can define your norm, please take time to pause and savor your achievements and surroundings. Many have said, life is not a sprint but a marathon. As we RTTR, if we are in too much of a hurry and we do not listen to those gentle prompts to tell us to stop, then we might arrive at the destination with emptiness in our ABCs. It would be a sad definition of our norm if we were to arrive and not have anyone there to enjoy it with us. The journey is where the stories are made and told, where the beliefs develop, and connections are forged so we can continue to RTTR.

Life is not a sprint but a marathon.

Let's make the most of our opportunities so that we are glad more often than sad. Crisis or significant change will reveal what our pockets have been filled with or, sadly, for some, that they are empty of the things that matter most in the end.

When we lose sight of our reference points, or lose sight of land, it is more difficult to discern that we are drifting. Drifting can result in being a danger to others as well as ourselves. Imagine being a ship that has sailed off its path and others, travelling through the night, did not expect to see anything in the vicinity. When they finally see the unexpected object, it is too late. It is the story of the Titanic. Just like marriage or parenting, when we are drifting, we lose those moments, those golden, teachable times that are so valuable. Those are the times that would bring about a smiling memory based in a do-you-remember-when kind of moment. Drifting too long will result in a wreck.

Addressing the ABCs using a PIES Formula and SMART Goals will address any unwanted drift we may experience. We can still have our moments of drifting but we remain in the boat and remain aware of our course so we can return to it when we are ready.

Decisions, Whether You Like It Or Not

The truth is that no decision is, in fact, a decision. Silence does not signify consent or disagreement; it signifies choosing to do nothing.

In the spring of 1883, two young men graduated from medical school. The two differed from one another in both appearance and ambition. Ben was short and stocky. Will was tall and thin. Ben dreamed of practicing medicine in a big city. Will wanted to work in a rural community. Ben begged his friend to go to New York where they could both make a fortune. Will refused. His friend called him foolish for wanting to practice medicine in the Midwest. "But," Will said, "I want first to be a great surgeon...the very best, if I have the ability." Years later the wealthy and powerful came from around the world to be treated by Will at his clinic in Rochester, MN, the *Mayo Clinic*.

No matter what you or I choose to do there will always be the 20,000 in the stands who are the experts at whatever it is we are doing. For every person who chooses to take an action there are others who have chosen to live according to their fears who will critique, criticize, and offer all kinds of different thoughts while they stand on the shore living a life that is not headed anywhere on purpose.

My Final Desire for You

If you are competing to thrive not just survive, if you want to Run Toward the Roar, if you are struggling to find a RTTR person in your life or if you have any questions, please contact me.

I guarantee that I will not stand on the shore filling your boat with *shoulds*, and *ought to's*. I will be more than willing to pull your boat ashore and fix some leaks, ensure you have the right people and/or gear with you, or maybe even climb in and help you to paddle so you can chart your course and learn strategies to get you where you want to go. This is one of my core values!

I know this sounds like an unusual way to end a book on thriving through crisis/change but, please don't quit – yes, get discouraged – but find that person or those people who will supply some more courage for you. Many have been taught not to use four-letter words, but please use one: *Help* is one four-letter word that I truly hope and pray you would be willing to use!

It is my deepest desire that you will define what you will be faithful to. To discover the kind of *faithfulness* in which you make a difference in the lives you have been called to serve. I only want to be faithful to encouraging others to RTTR, so you finish the race, and you finish well.

Remember **passio fidelis:** passion and faithfulness; and that's my desire: that you find the passion and faithfulness to your values.

It is not possible to read or hear about resilience and thriving in a book or in a classroom and become resilient and thrive. Resilience is a quality, a characteristic of a person, which is developed and grown. It is not something we study to reiterate during a test, but it *is* a practice we can learn, pursue, and develop so that we grow stronger and improve our life and others'.

It all starts with a conversation.

Let's Talk?

ENDNOTES

1   Rochester, S. and Kiley, F. (1998). *Honor Bound: The History of American Prisoners of War in Southeast Asia, 1961-1973*. Office of the Secretary of Defense, Historical Office. 413.

2   https://www.rsph.org.uk/

3   https://www.psychalive.org/worst-mental-health-instagram-facebook-youtube

4   Berman, J. (Producer) & Russell, M.D. (Director). (2011). *Seven Days in Utopia*. [Motion Picture]. United States: Prospect Park & Utopia Pictures.

5   Hendricks, S. (2016.09.30). *Free Will or Free Won't. Neuroscience on the Choices We Can (and Can't) Make*. https://bigthink.com/scotty-hendricks/free-will-or-free-wont-what-neuroscience-says-about-the-choices-we-can-and-cant-make.

6   Clarke, P. (2013). *The Libet Experiment and Its Implications for Free Will. From* https://www.bethinking.org/human-life/the-libet-experiment-and-its-implications-for-conscious-will.

7   Miller, D. (June 3, 2020). *Donald Miller Teaches Productivity*. Livestream Event https://storybrand.com/donald-miller-teaches-productivity-june-2020/.

8   Carver. C. (1998). Resilience and Thriving: Issues, Models, and Linkages. *Journal of Social Issues, 52(4)*, 245-266.

9   Ernst, R., Reed, S. & Welle V. (August 2018). *Lesson Plan: Practicing Resilience*. From https://www.apa.org/ed/precollege/topss/teaching-resources/practicing-resilience-lesson.

10 American Psychological Association. (2012). *Building Your Resilience*. https://www.apa.org/topics/resilience/.

11 Webster's Revised Unabridged Dictionary. https://www.merriam-webster.com/dictionary/thrive.

12 Online Etymology Dictionary. https://www.etymonline.com/word/thrive.

13 Drucker, P. (January 2005). *Managing Oneself*. Harvard Business Review Press. https://hbr.org/2005/01/managing-oneself.

14 Meade, M. (2011 August 19). *Go Toward The Roar*. https://www.huffpost.com/entry/facing-your-fears_b_928300#:~:text=The%20old%20lions%20go%20off,hungry%20lions%20wait%20and%20watch.&text=As%20they%20rush%20wildly%20in,to%20tell%20the%20young%20ones.

15 Merriam-Webster Dictionary. https://www.merriam-webster.com/dictionary/ethos.

16 n.a. (2019 March 26). *Elements of Writing in the Professional World.* https://business-writing731601800.wordpress.com/.

17 Online Etymology Dictionary. *Origin and meaning of Passion.* https://www.etymonline.com/word/passion.

18 Liddell, H. & Scott, R. (n.d.). *An Intermediate Greek-English Lexicon.* http://www.perseus.tufts.edu/hopper/text?doc=Perseus:text:1999.04.0058:entry%3Dlo/gos.

19 Kennedy, G. (1991). *Aristotle On Rhetoric: A Theory of Civic Discourse.* New York: Oxford University Press.

20 Bible Hub. (n.d.). *2920 Krisis.* https://biblehub.com/greek/2920.htm.

21 Venette, S.J. (2003). *Risk Communication in a High Reliability Organization.* Ann Arbor, MI. UMI Proquest Information and Learning.

22 Ibid. Venette (2003).

23 The Free Dictionary. https://www.thefreedictionary.com/refinable.

24 Krause, J. (n.d.). *The History and Evolution of SMART Goals.* https://www.achieveit.com/resources/blog/the-history-and-evolution-of-smart-goals

25 New American Standard Bible. *Hebrews 11:1.* https://biblehub.com/nasb/hebrews/11.htm.

26 Browning, R. (1855). *Men and Women.* https://www.gutenberg.org/files/17393/17393-h/17393-h.htm#link2H_4_0009.

27 Roosevelt, T. (April 23, 1910). *The Man in the Arena: Citizenship in a Republic.* https://theodoreroosevelt.org/content.aspx?page_id=22&club_id=991271&module_id=339364.

28 Niebuhr, R. & McAfee Brown, R. (2009). *The Essential Reinhold Niebuhr: Selected Essays and Addresses.* London, UK: Yale University Press, 251.

29 Good News Translation. *Proverbs, 4:23.* https://www.biblegateway.com/passage/?-search=Proverbs+4&version=GNT.

30 https://www.brainyquote.com/quotes/marcus_aurelius_148747.

31 https://www.britannica.com/topic/cogito-ergo-sum.

32 https://www.quoteslyfe.com.

33 https://www.brainyquote.com/quotes/ralph_waldo_emerson_108797.

34 http://www.quotationspage.com/quotes/William_James.

35 Ellis, A. (2002). *Rational Emotive Behavior Therapy. Encyclopedia of Psychotherapy.* 2. 483-487. USA: Elsevier Science.

36 Collins, J. (2001). *Good to Great: Why Some Companies Make the Leap...and Others Don't.* New York: Harper Business. 85.

37 Rochester, S. & Kiley, F. (1998). *Honor Bound: The History of American Prisoners of War in Southeast Asia, 1961-1973.* Office of the Secretary of Defense, Historical Office. 413.

38 https://www.goodreads.com/quotes/267482-the-longer-i-live-the-more-i-realize-the-impact.

39 Frankl, V. (2019). *Man's Search for Meaning*. Toronto, ON: Random House Canada. 86.

40 Hogg, M., & Vaughan, G. (2005). Social Psychology (4th edition). London: Prentice-Hall. 150.

41 New Living Translation. *Philippians 3:13-14*. https://biblehub.com/nlt/philippians/3.htm.

42 Ziglar, Z. (October 6, 1997, rev'd ed.). *Over The Top*. Nashville: Thomas Nelson, Inc.

43 Wheeler, M. (n.d.). *Emotions, Feelings, and Moods: What's the Difference?* https://www.6seconds.org/2017/05/15/emotion-feeling-mood/.

44 New Living Translation Proverbs 25:20 NLT - https://www.biblegateway.com/passage/?search=Proverbs+25%3A20&version=NLT

45 Kincaid, Z. (February 22, 2019). *There Is No Safe Investment*. https://www.cslewis.com/no-safe-investment.

46 https://www.brainyquote.com/quotes/winston_churchill_103788.

47 The Living Bible. *James 1:6-8*.

48 Although often attributed to Albert Einstein, the origin of this saying/quote is not known.

49 Contemporary English Version. *Proverbs 4:23*. https://biblehub.com/proverbs/4-23.htm.

50 New American Standard Bible. *Proverbs 23:7*. https://biblehub.com/proverbs/23-7.htm.

51 Gandi, Mahatma. https://quotefancy.com/quote/1941/Mahatma-Gandhi-A-man-is-but-the-product-of-his-thoughts-What-he-thinks-he-becomes

52 Buddha https://duckduckgo.com/?t=ffsb&q=The+mind+is+everything%3A+what+you+think+you+become.+quote&atb=v261-1&iax=images&ia=images&iai=https%3A%2F%2Fcdn4.geckoandfly.com%2Fwp-content%2Fuploads%2F2014%2F04%2Fbuddha-buddhism-quote-religion7.jpg.

53 Descartes, Renee. https://duckduckgo.com/?t=ffsb&q=I+think+therefore+I+AM+QUOTE&atb=v261-1&iax=images&ia=images&iai=https%3A%2F%2Fi.pinimg.com%2Foriginals%2F80%2Fc4%2Fed%2F80c4ed78649c809c3c3b3b5ca658500a.jpg.

54 Emerson, Ralph Waldo. https://www.brainyquote.com/quotes/ralph_waldo_emerson_108797.

55 James, W. J. (October 1895). *Is Life Worth Living? International Journal of Ethics*, 6:1. 24.

56 Dr. Albert Ellis developed the REBT approach—Rational Emotional Behavioural Therapy. The fundamental assertion of REBT is that the way people feel is largely influenced by how they think. See Cherry, K. (June 20, 2019). *How Rational Emotive Behavior Therapy Works*. https://www.verywellmind.com/rational-emotive-behavior-therapy-2796000.

57 Collins, J. (2001). *Good to Great: Why Some Companies Make the Leap ... and Others Don't.* New York: Harper Business.

58 Seligman, M.E.P. (2006). *Learned Optimism: How to Change Your Mind and Your Life.* UK: Vintage.

59 Bandura, A. Ramachaudran, V.S. (Ed). (1994). Self-efficacy. *Encyclopedia of Human Behavior.* 4. 71-81. New York: Academic Press.

60 Bandura, A. (1997). *Self-efficacy: The exercise of control.* W H Freeman/Times Book/ Henry Holt & Co.

61 Rotter, J. B. (1966). Generalized expectancies for internal versus external control of reinforcement. *Psychology Monogr.* 80, 1–28.

62 New Revived Standard Version. Romans 5:3-5. https://www.bible.com/bible/2016/ ROM.5.3-5.NRSV.

63 Stockstill, J. (January 16, 2017). *How Does Suffering Lead To Hope? You Might Be Surprised.* https://medium.com/@joelstockstill/how-does-suffering-lead-to-hope-you-may-be-surprised-46272093152b.

64 New Living Translations. Romans 8:28. https://www.biblegateway.com/passage/?-search=Romans%208:28&version=NLT.

65 The Reticular Activating System refers to a diffuse network of nerve pathways in the brainstem connecting the spinal cord, cerebrum, and cerebellum, and mediating the overall level of consciousness.

66 Smedes, L. (1984). *Forgive and Forget: Healing the Hurts We Don't Deserve.* https:// www.goodreads.com/author/quotes/56576.Lewis_B_Smedes.

67 Ibid. Smedes (1984).

68 International Standard Version. *Timothy 6:9.* https://biblehub.com/isv/1_timothy/ 6.htm.

69 University of Missouri-Columbia. (August 20, 2012). *Spirituality correlates to better mental health regardless of religion, says MU researchers.* https://www.eurekalert. org/news-releases/549286.

70 New International Version. *Hebrews 11:1.* https://www.biblegateway.com/pas-sage/?search=Hebrews%2011%3A1&version=NIV.

71 English Standard Version. *Corinthians 4:18.* https://biblehub.com/esv/2_corinthi-ans/4.htm.

72 Hamilton, G. (April 13, 2017). *Canadians May Be Vacating the Pews but They Are Keeping the Faith: Poll.* https://nationalpost.com/news/canada/canadians-may-be-vacating-the-pews-but-they-are-keeping-the-faith-poll.

73 Teirney, J. and Baumeister, R. (2019). *The Power of Bad: How The Negativity Effect Rules Us And How We Can Rule It.* New York: Penguin Press.

74 Reivich, K. & Shatte, A. (2003) *The Resilience Factor: 7 Keys to Finding Your Inner Strength and Overcoming Life's Hurdles.* New York: Broadway Books.

[75] Dweck, C.S. (2006). *Mindset: The New Psychology of Success*. New York: Random House.

[76] Davis, K. (1996). *How To Speak to Youth...And Keep Them Awake at The Same Time: A Step-By-Step Guide To Improving Your Talks*. Grand Rapids, MI: Vonderzan. 104-106.

[77] C.S. Lewis. (1960). *The Four Loves*. New York City: Harcourt Brace.

[78] Gus Lee, G. & Elliott-Lee, D. (2006). *Courage: The Backbone of Leadership*. San Francisco: Josey-Boss. 149.

[79] New American Standard Bible. *Galatians 6:1* https://biblehub.com/nasb_/galatians/6.htm.

[80] Sarason, I.G., Sarason, B.R., Shearin, E.N. & Pierce, G.R. (1987). A Brief Measure of Social Support: Practical and Theoretical Implications. *Journal of Social and Personal Relationships*. 4:4. 497–510.

[81] To take this questionnaire, go to fortlog.co/runtowardstheroar and you will find the Purdue Social Support Scale in PDF form for easier future reference. You can also find other versions online – it is a free tool.

[82] House, J.S., Landis, K.R. & Umberson, K.R. (July 29, 1988). Social relationships and health. *Science* 241:4865. 540-545.

[83] Miller, M., Smith-Lovin, L. & Brashears, M.E. (June 1, 2006. Social Isolation in America: Changes in Core Discussion Networks over Two Decades. American Sociological Review. 71. 353-375.

[84] Powell, J. (1999). *Why Am I Afraid to Tell You Who I Am?* Grand Rapids, MI: Zondervan.

[85] Gottman J.M. (1999). *The Seven Principles for Making Marriage Work: A Practical Guide from the Country's Foremost Relationship Expert*. New York: Harmony Books.

[86] Chapman, G. (2015)., *The Five Love Languages: The Secret to Love that Lasts*. Chicago: Northfield Publishing.

[87] Kidder, R. M. (2006). Moral Courage. New York: William Morrow Paperbacks. 72.

[88] Syme, S.L. (January 1, 2006). Social Determinants of Health: The Community as Empowered Partner. *Preventing Chronic Disease*. 1:1. A02.

[89] New American Standard Bible 1995. *Proverbs 22:6*. https://www.biblegateway.com/passage/?search=Proverbs+22%3A6&version=NASB1995.

[90] KLTV. (November 6, 2009). 5:47 PM CST. East Texas

[91] Katila, B. (June 1, 2019). *The Unexamined Life Is Not Worth Living*. https://www.godslivingstones.org/all-content/the-unexamined-life-is-not-worth-living/a632.

[92] English Standard Version. Proverbs 3:13. https://www.biblegateway.com/passage/?search=Proverbs+3%3A13&version=ESV

[93] New International Version 1984.Proverbs 4:7. https://www.studylight.org/bible/eng/n84/proverbs/4.html.

[94] Stone, L. (November 30, 2009). Beyond Simple Multi-tasking: Continuous Partial Attention. https://lindastone.net/2009/11/30/beyond-simple-multi-tasking-continuous-partial-attention/.

ABOUT THE AUTHOR

John Robertson is a workforce wellness expert and culture alignment specialist with over 30 years of experience helping organizations and individuals navigate crises.

John works with forward-thinking organizations and leaders to do four things:

- Transform their Traditional Crisis Response
- Reframe Wellness Practically
- Develop a refined approach for mental wellness
- Create Leaders and Workforces that are Engaged and Thrive

This is done with the RUN TOWARD THE ROAR ETHOS. After all, business works when people thrive.

Inspired and driven by his values, John acts as a facilitator for his clients as they test, discover, and expand what they can do. He uses concrete, verifiable processes to help them achieve demonstrable, solution-focused results. Remaining faithful to his passions and values, John invests himself in his vocation without reservation. He provides spirit-filled, insightful guidance that his clients use to amplify their lives and their businesses. John truly provides "leadership that people can follow through storms."

Connect with John at www.fortlog.co.

Manufactured by Amazon.ca
Bolton, ON

24622252R00125